A Palestinian State

Written under the auspices of the Center for Strategic Studies,
Tel-Aviv University

A Palestinian State
The Implications for Israel

Mark A. Heller

Harvard University Press
Cambridge, Massachusetts, and London, England   1983

10 9 8 7 6 5 4 3 2

This book is printed on acid-free paper, and its binding
materials have been chosen for strength and durability.

Library of Congress Cataloging in Publication Data

Heller, Mark.
    A Palestinian state.

    Bibliography: p.
    Includes index.
    1.   Jewish-Arab relations — 1973–
    2.   Palestine — Politics and government — 1948–
    I.   Title.
DS119.7.H3855 1983   956'.04   82–15698
ISBN 0–674–65221–5

for the children

Preface

Analyses of contemporary Middle Eastern politics are notoriously perishable. Government policies are frequently declared, and sometimes reversed, with dramatic effect, regional alignments shift with impressive abruptness, and leading personalities may disappear suddenly from the scene. The volatility of the region was demonstrated, once again, by three noteworthy events in the first half of September 1982. During that period, President Ronald Reagan expressed an American preference for Palestinian self-government in the West Bank and Gaza Strip, in association with Jordan; Arab leaders, previously unable to overcome their political differences, met in Fez, Morocco, and coupled their traditional demand for an independent Palestinian state with a vaguely worded peace plan which was later interpreted by King Husayn of Jordan to portend recognition of Israel; and Bashir Jumayyil, the president-elect of Lebanon, was assassinated nine days before he was scheduled to assume office.

The turbulence of those two weeks, though unusual in its intensity, is hardly atypical of Middle Eastern politics, and it is therefore not surprising that published writings, by the time they have gone through the production process, often appear to have been outmoded by intervening developments. Unfortunately, there is little reason to hope that the present study, before it is published, will have been rendered obsolete by solutions to the problems it attempts to address.

This analysis was completed before the Israeli invasion of Lebanon in June 1982. The Israeli campaign dealt the Palestine

Liberation Organization (PLO) a severe military blow, deprived it of the protostate it had built up in southern Lebanon, and compelled it to abandon its political base of operations in Beirut. Nevertheless, the PLO has not been destroyed, and it has emerged from the war in Lebanon with its prestige intact. Whether or not this will be a transitory outcome cannot be foreseen. But whatever the institutional fate of the PLO, the "Palestine problem" has not been resolved in a manner that can restore stability to Lebanon, produce a viable, long-term status for the West Bank and Gaza, normalize Israel's relations with the rest of the Arab world, or alleviate the economic, diplomatic, and social burdens imposed on Israel by the state of war. Furthermore, even if the PLO ceases to exist in its present form, Israel will almost certainly have to contend with some other manifestation of Palestinian collective consciousness.

Indeed, far from making the analysis obsolete, current developments may cause it to be even more relevant to the policy agenda, because the exercise is predicated on a fundamental change in the Palestinian position on the conflict, and the war in Lebanon may finally disabuse the PLO—or any successor organization—of the notion that maximalist goals are ever attainable, or that violent means can secure any goals at all. Furthermore, with the PLO's infrastructure crippled and Syria's military reputation tarnished, many Israelis may also be more assured about the balance of power in the region, and therefore assess differently the relative risks and opportunities of various political alternatives. It is, of course, difficult to predict how—if at all—the political fluidities created by events in Lebanon will be exploited, but debate on the issues will inevitably continue, perhaps giving rise to serious negotiations, and it is hoped that the ideas presented here will contribute to that process.

Any treatment of an issue as emotionally charged as the Israeli-Arab conflict demands some clarification of the author's perspective. I make no pretense at impartiality. My primary concern throughout is Israel's security and well-being, defined to include certain social, political, and moral components in addition to military imperatives. But while I am not a disinterested observer, I have consciously attempted to examine strategies—

the means by which objectives may be pursued — in as rational a fashion as possible. Analysis, of course, can never be completely divorced from subjective concerns, but the effort to understand reality without sentimental or mythological prisms must still be made if policy is to be planned with maximum effectiveness.

This goal is reflected in the effort to avoid value-laden terminology. Place-names, for example, are controversial because they are often taken as implicit endorsement of the legitimacy of ownership claims by one side or the other to the conflict. In this study, conventional English usage is generally adopted, but names preferred by Jews or Arabs are intended to be interchangeable, in both text and maps, with no normative connotation. "Palestine" and "Eretz Yisrael" both refer to the 26,000 square kilometers of former Ottoman lands between the River Jordan and the Mediterranean that were demarcated as a separate territorial-political entity after World War I. Similarly, "the West Bank" and "Judaea and Samaria" denote that part of east-central Palestine which came under Jordanian control in 1948 and was captured by Israel in 1967. Rigorous application of the principal of terminological positivism would entail the modification of the term "Palestinian" whenever it is applied to people, since it can describe Jews as well as Arabs, but for reasons of economy, "Palestinian," unless otherwise specified, refers only to Palestinian Arabs.

One result of this approach is that some readers have characterized the tone of the study as almost clinical. This is a criticism to which I happily plead guilty. The historical, religious, and ideological passions surrounding the creation of Israel and the Israeli-Arab conflict are too blatant to be ignored and yet too well known to require repetition; they are part of the environment. Still, it is the obligation of policy analysts to ensure that these passions do not paralyze thought. Without the first, action is meaningless; without the second, it is futile.

Although I bear sole responsibility for the opinions expressed here, many others helped bring this book to fruition. I am very gratified that it is being published under the auspices of the Center for Strategic Studies, Tel-Aviv University. Since 1979, the

CSS has provided, not just an institutional home, but intellectual challenge, friendship, and support in occasionally difficult times. The Head of the CSS, Major General (Res.) Aharon Yariv, has given encouragement in word and deed, solved every crisis that arose, and reminded me of what people mean when they say "mensch." Aryeh Shalev forced me to question everything I wrote and to consider things I did not. Our discussions generated much heat, though perhaps not as much light as he would wish, and his help is very much appreciated. Others at the CSS contributed ideas and criticism. Without intending to slight any of them, I want to acknowledge the special efforts of two colleagues and friends. Shai Feldman supplied a responsive sounding board early on and very useful comments on the first draft. The late Avi Plascov gave me a generous share of the time remaining in his too-short life in order to deepen my understanding of a subject he knew well and help me clarify my own thoughts. I believe that he would have approved of the final version. Thanks are due as well to the CSS administrative staff, especially to Executive Editor Joseph Alpher and to Moshe Grundman, head of the Documentation Center, who responded, despite political misgivings, to requests for more "ammunition" with grace and unfailing good humor.

I also benefited from the insights of scholars outside the CSS — Shlomo Gazit, Aaron Klieman, Shaul Mishal, Elie Rekhess, Eliyahu Kanovsky, and Nadav Safran — who took time from their busy schedules to read part or all of the manuscript. The maps were done by Haim Zvi Carmel. His cartographic skills are self-evident, but his patience with a sometimes confused author deserves special mention. At Harvard University Press, I found tolerance, courtesy, and a constant desire to help. I would particularly like to acknowledge the support of Aida Donald and Elizabeth Suttell, whose guidance and editorial skills transformed the manuscript into something better.

And then there is Barbi, my wife and partner, in this as in all things. No words —

M.A.H.
September 1982

Contents

Maps

Tables

A Palestinian State

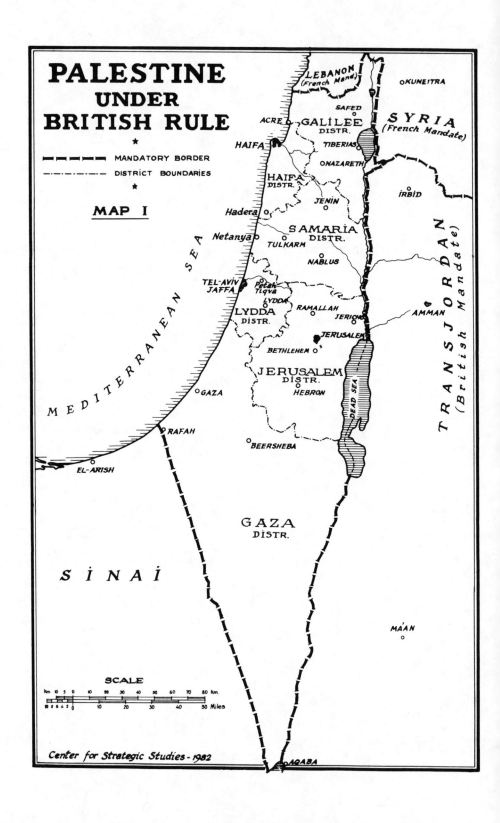

PALESTINE
UNDER
BRITISH RULE

★

▬ ▬ ▬ ▬ ▬ MANDATORY BORDER

▬·▬·▬·▬ DISTRICT BOUNDARIES

★

MAP I

LEBANON
(French Mand.)

OKUNEITRA

SAFED ○

ACRE ○ GALILEE
DISTR.

SYRIA
(French Mandate)

HAIFA ○ TIBERIAS ○

○ NAZARETH

HAIFA
DISTR.

IRBID ○

JENIN ○

Hadera ○

Netanya ○ SAMARIA
DISTR.

TULKARM ○

NABLUS ○

TEL-AVIV
JAFFA

Petah
Tiqva ○

LYDDA ○

RAMALLAH ○

JERICHO ○

AMMAN ♥

LYDDA
DISTR.

JERUSALEM

BETHLEHEM ○

JERUSALEM
DISTR.

HEBRON ○

GAZA ○

RAFAH ○

EL-ARISH ○

BEERSHEBA ○

M E D I T E R R A N E A N   S E A

DEAD SEA

T R A N S J O R D A N
(British Mandate)

GAZA
DISTR.

S I N A I

MA'AN ○

SCALE

Km. 10 5 0   10   20   30   40   50   60   70   80 km.

10 8 6 4 2 0   10   20   30   40   50 Miles

Center for Strategic Studies - 1982

○ AQABA

1

Introduction

The political objective of Zionism, since its emergence in the late nineteenth century, has been the renewal of an independent Jewish national existence in Palestine. During the last decades of Ottoman rule, some important institutional achievements were registered, but the most significant political breakthrough came after World War I, when Palestine was placed under the administration of a British mandatory government officially committed to Zionist aspirations. For the next thirty years, British governments pursued an inconsistent policy that permitted the development of a Jewish economic and social infrastructure in the country but frequently complicated the pursuit of Zionism's central political goal. The greatest challenge to the Zionist enterprise, however, was the existence of a separate Arab national movement in Palestine, which claimed exclusive possession of and control over the same territory (Map I) and which benefitted from the support, in varying degrees, of other Arab communities and states in the Middle East.

The struggle between these two rival movements constituted the "question of Palestine," and its first phase terminated in 1948, when British rule in Palestine came to an end and the Jewish national movement prevailed in the "civil war" between Palestinian Arabs and Palestinian Jews. The Jewish assertion of statehood was immediately contested by invading armies from the neighboring Arab states, but in the ensuing war Israel was able to consolidate its independence and to extend its authority over all of mandatory Palestine except for approximately 5,600 square kilometers in east-central Palestine (the West Bank),

Kab... — self contained isolated Jewish communities [handwritten marginalia]

subsequently annexed by Jordan, and a small wedge of about 360 square kilometers in the southwest (the Gaza Strip), which came under Egyptian military administration. Israel was unable, however, to convince or compel the Palestinian Arabs and the rest of the Arab world to accept the legitimacy or finality of Jewish statehood. The armistice agreements that ended the fighting in 1949 (Map II) were not converted into peace treaties, and no political resolution of the question of Palestine was achieved. Since then, Israel has faced a permanent security threat in the form of unremitting Arab hostility.

The Palestinian Arabs themselves, their social structures and political institutions shattered during the turbulence of 1947–1949, ceased to be a major political factor in the conflict, at least until the creation of the Palestine Liberation Organization (PLO) in 1964. But their cause was upheld by various Arab states whose military power represented a continuing danger to Israel. Furthermore, the issues in the Arab-Israeli conflict ramified, as disputes with individual Arab states over territory, water, and rights of passage were grafted onto the original question of Palestine. On various occasions, Arab hostility produced actual war coalitions, although the composition of these coalitions fluctuated over time, as did the material and psychological effort their members were willing or able to invest in the confrontation with Israel.

Until President Anwar Sadat's visit to Jerusalem in 1977, however, irreconcilable Arab hostility was taken as a fundamental datum, and Israel was forced to rely primarily on a "single-track" strategy of capacity maximization in order to cope with the security threat. Optimum use of the human, material, territorial, and diplomatic assets at Israel's disposal, and their enhancement where possible, were intended to deter or else frustrate Arab efforts to undermine Israel's security. If the Arab military potential was never fully realized, this was a fortuitous outcome for Israel, resulting from inter-Arab rivalries, domestic upheavals, or structural dislocations in the Arab states, rather than from Israeli political initiatives. The 1979 peace treaty with Egypt represents the first instance of a "double-track" strategy —one that combines elements of capacity maximization with

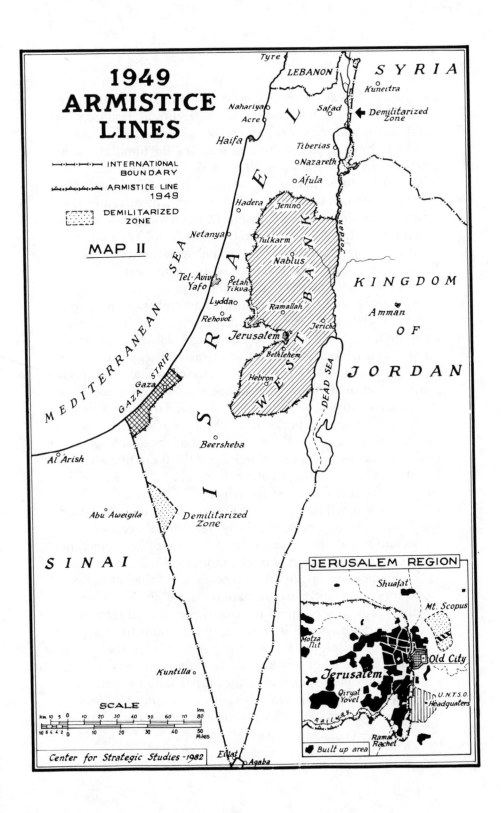

1949 ARMISTICE LINES

⊢·⊣·⊢·⊣ INTERNATIONAL BOUNDARY
⊢·⊣·⊢·⊣ ARMISTICE LINE 1949
▦ DEMILITARIZED ZONE

MAP II

MEDITERRANEAN SEA

LEBANON
SYRIA
Tyre
Kuneitra
Nahariya
Acre
Safad
← Demilitarized Zone
Haifa
Tiberias
Nazareth
Afula
Hadera
Jenino
Netanya
Tulkarm
Nablus
Tel-Aviv Yafo
Petah Tikva
Lyddao
Ramallah
Amman
Rehovot
Jericho
Jerusalem
Bethlehem
Hebron
WEST BANK
KINGDOM
OF
JORDAN
DEAD SEA

I S R A E L

Gaza
GAZA STRIP

Al Arish

Beersheba

Abu Aweigila
Demilitarized Zone

S I N A I

Kuntilla

JERUSALEM REGION

Shuafat
Mt. Scopus
Motza Illit
Old City
Jerusalem
Qiryat Yovel
U.N.T.S.O. Headquaters
Railway
Rama Rachel

■ Built up area

SCALE
Km. 10 5 0   10   20   30   40   50   60   70   80 km.
10 8 6 4 2 0   10   20   30   40   50 Miles

Eilat
Aqaba

Center for Strategic Studies -1982

elements of threat reduction, pursued through political means intended, even at the cost of some territorial resources, to diminish the collective Arab incentive to prosecute the conflict.

The purpose of this study is to examine the implications for Israel of the continued pursuit of a double-track strategy on other fronts. In particular, the object is to evaluate the impact on Israel's national security of a peace settlement centered on Israeli agreement to the establishment of an independent Palestinian state in the West Bank and the Gaza Strip. The evaluation is based on assessments of the probable nature of threats to Israeli interests and the capacity of Israel to deal with those threats in the aftermath of such a settlement.

Any analysis of this type confronts a number of limitations. The most obvious is that even the possibility of formal peace based on the establishment of a Palestinian state is, at this stage, purely hypothetical. A double-track Israeli strategy with respect to Egypt was feasible only after it became clear that the terms of peace, rather than the principle of peace itself, were at issue. But the declared objective of the PLO, as defined in the Palestine National Charter and periodically reaffirmed by resolutions of the Palestine National Council and pronouncements of PLO leaders and constituent organizations, is the total "liberation" of Palestine, that is, the elimination of Israel as a political entity. This was the stated purpose for which the PLO was founded — when the West Bank and Gaza were in Arab, not Israeli, hands — and it has been regularly reaffirmed ever since by authoritative Palestinian institutions.[1] In what has sometimes been interpreted as a sign of moderation, the PLO has expressed its "willingness" to create an "independent combatant national authority" or an "independent national state" in any "liberated territory," but only on condition that this not entail recognition of or peace with Israel.[2] It is therefore important to emphasize that this study explores, not a current option, but rather the implications for Israel of a policy whose viability is contingent on a marked shift in the position of the Palestinians and their Arab supporters. The present analysis does not attempt to assess the likelihood that this shift will be forthcoming, but only the probable impact on Israel's strategic situation if a settlement made possible by such a shift were somehow to materialize.

A second limitation applies to the confidence with which the consequences of policy choices can be foreseen. Even if it is assumed, for analytical purposes, that such a settlement is attainable, the implications of a Palestinian state remain highly speculative. The behavior of this state would be very much conditioned by its domestic structures and the quality of its relations with other regional and extraregional actors, in addition to its own autonomous preferences. Given the inherent uncertainties of social, economic, demographic, and political development and the fluidities of interstate relations in the Arab world, any characterization of the anticipated impact of a peace settlement based on an independent Palestinian state must be probabilistic. Furthermore, the strategic value to Israel of such an outcome — its costs and benefits, risks and opportunities — is purely relative. It must be assessed, not in isolation, but in comparison with the value of other possible postures. No strategy recommends itself solely on its intrinsic merits and demerits, but only in relation to other available strategies, including efforts to perpetuate the status quo. Unfortunately, the factors involved in a comparative analysis of this sort do not lend themselves to precise measurement. Instead, they permit only qualitative estimates, the accuracy of which can never be known, even ex post facto, and policy prescriptions that flow from such estimates should therefore display a corresponding modesty.

The main conclusion of this study is that a settlement based on an independent Palestinian state which meets certain minimal conditions actually constitutes a recommended strategic choice for Israel, because its combined threat minimization–capacity maximization value, while not high, is superior to that of the other, even less appealing, alternatives. The minimal conditions are:

(1) the Palestinian state will be part of a general settlement of the "Palestine problem" which will also resolve other

outstanding issues (refugees, property claims, and so forth) and which will provide for a peace treaty and normal relations between Israel and the Palestinian state;

(2) the peace settlement will be negotiated directly by Israel and the authoritative spokesman of the Palestinian national movement, that is, the Palestine Liberation Organization, or any body that might succeed it;

(3) the peace settlement will be ratified at least by the most critical Arab states — Jordan, Saudi Arabia, and perhaps Syria, in addition to Egypt — and will be accompanied by the establishment of normal relations of peace between Israel and these states;

(4) the Palestinian state will accept certain verifiable restrictions on force levels, military equipment, and troop deployment, as well as on military relations with other states;

(5) the territorial settlement will be based on the 1949 armistice lines, with the possibility of minor rectifications and a special regime for Jerusalem;

(6) the implementation of the peace settlement will be gradual, with the transition period lasting five to ten years.

The value to Israel of a Palestine-state settlement would be determined, of course, by its specific character rather than by its mere existence. It is entirely conceivable that a peace settlement could be achieved that did not meet these minimal conditions, in which case it would probably not be advisable. It is also possible that even more reassuring provisions could be secured, in which case the relative value to Israel would be further enhanced. Diplomacy alone can determine whether specific conditions are attainable. The policy analyst must assume their presence or absence in order to evaluate the implications.

The task of assessing the implications of a settlement based on an independent Palestinian state is thus further complicated, but the need to address the subject nevertheless remains. This is so, not just because it is very much on the international agenda, but also because the uncertainties involved apply in equal measure to any other conceivable policy choice for Israel, including the status quo. Failure to explore the subject thoroughly means only that some other policy of no less probabilistic strategic value will be pursued, but with no demonstrable basis for believing that it is preferable to the roads not taken.

2

Israel's Security Dilemma

During the second historical phase of the Arab-Israeli conflict, from 1948 to 1967, a state of armed truce prevailed between Israel and its Arab neighbors. Despite the existence of various armistice and cease-fire agreements, Arab-Israeli relations were characterized by recurring violence — infiltration and sabotage by Arab terrorists, Israeli retaliatory raids, Syrian-Israeli exchanges of fire, a major clash between Egypt and Israel in 1956 — and, most critically, the permanent possibility of renewed full-scale war. Given uncompromising Arab hostility and the refusal to consider a political settlement of the conflict under any terms, Israeli policymakers had no choice but to follow a single-track strategy — to strive for maximal military preparedness.

The costs of a single-track strategy

The economic and demographic imbalance in favor of the Arab states made an intense exploitation of Israel's material and manpower resources necessary in order to underwrite an acceptable military balance. Even before 1967, Israel's defense effort, at least as reflected in security-related expenditures, was quite high by world standards. The burden, however, was still well within Israel's economic capacity to bear. Indeed, defense outlays in the range of 8-11 percent of gross national product were actually accompanied by high levels of investment, continuous improvements in the relative balance of payments (proportion of imports financed by exports), and rapid population increases, all combining to produce the highest long-term rate of economic growth in the world.[1]

After the Six Day War of 1967, this situation began to change. On the one hand, Israel's overwhelming military victory left it in possession of additional territories that conferred significant military assets — shorter land frontiers (but a longer coastline) to defend, physical obstacles to Arab assaults (water barriers at the Suez Canal and Jordan River, a line of hills on the Golan Heights), and greater strategic depth on all fronts (Map III). Greater depth also entailed longer lines of supply and communication, especially in the Sinai, but this impediment was minor compared to the advantages that control of the territories provided.

On the other hand, the very magnitude of Israel's achievement also changed the quality of Arab-Israeli relations and ushered in a third, more intense, phase of the conflict. By discrediting Gamal 'Abd al-Nasir, the personification of the pan-Arab cause, and simultaneously ejecting Arab rule from those parts of mandatory Palestine that had been "saved" in 1948 from Jewish control, the Israeli victory contributed to the revivification of particularistic Palestinian consciousness and the international saliency of the Palestine-national cause. One immediate consequence was an increase in armed infiltration into Israeli-administered territory and in shelling incidents from across the cease-fire lines. An even weightier threat emerged from the determination of the Arab confrontation states — Egypt, Syria, and, to a lesser extent, Jordan — to renew armed conflict at the earliest appropriate moment. In comparison with the pre-1967 situation, these states were far less willing to tolerate the status quo, even in the short run, not only because it was a constant reminder of the humiliation they had experienced, but also because its territorial outcome represented an immediate and direct stimulus to action, rather than just a derivative grievance produced by Arab solidarity with the Palestinians. Thus, Arab decisionmakers undertook the risks and costs of a military expansion that required, in turn, a continuous enhancement of Israel's capacity. The territories, alone, could not provide this

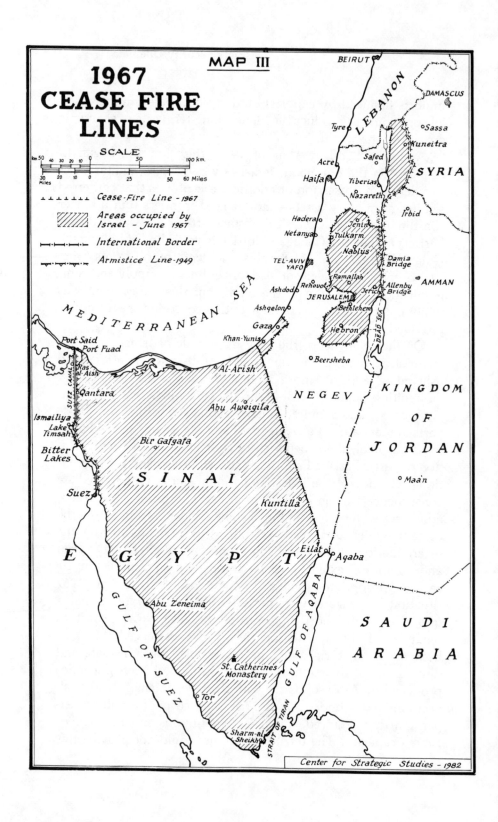

MAP III

1967
CEASE FIRE
LINES

SCALE

km 50 40 30 20 10   50   100 km.

30 20 10 0   25   50   60 Miles
Miles

⊥⊥⊥⊥⊥⊥   Cease-Fire Line - 1967

▨▨▨   Areas occupied by
         Israel - June 1967

├─┼─┤   International Border

├╌┼╌┤   Armistice Line - 1949

BEIRUT

LEBANON

DAMASCUS

Tyre

Sassa

Kuneitra

Acre   Safed

SYRIA

Haifa   Tiberias

Nazareth   Irbid

Hadera   Jenin

Netanya   Tulkarm

TEL-AVIV-   Nablus   Damia
YAFO   Bridge

Rehovot   Ramallah   AMMAN
Ashdod   Jericho Allenby
        JERUSALEM   Bridge
Ashqelon   Bethlehem

Gaza   Hebron

Khan-Yunis

MEDITERRANEAN SEA

Beersheba

Port Said
Port Fuad

Ras   Al-Arish
al-Aish

NEGEV   KINGDOM

Qantara

Ismailiya   Abu Aweigila   OF
Lake
Timsah
Bitter   Bir Gafgafa   JORDAN
Lakes

Suez   S I N A I

Ma'an

Kuntilla

E   G   Y   P   T

Eilat Aqaba

SAUDI

Abu Zeneima

ARABIA

GULF OF SUEZ

GULF OF AQABA

St. Catherine's
Monastery

Tor

STRAIT OF TIRAN

Sharm-al-
Sheikh

DEAD SEA

Center for Strategic Studies - 1982

enhancement, and Israel's relative defense burden therefore increased sharply. From 1968 to 1972, defense outlays averaged
22 percent of GNP. Even during this period, the defense burden
was not inconsistent with impressive economic growth, including significant growth in domestic investment.[2] But a source
of longer-term concern was the fact that much of this growth,
unlike that of the pre-1967 period, was fueled by a growing
trade deficit financed, to an accelerating degree, by foreign
loans, with the result that Israel's foreign debt increased by an
unprecedented 137 percent in this five-year period — well more
than double the rate of growth in GNP.[3]

Nevertheless, the problems of this period pale in comparison
with those of the post-Yom Kippur War era. Since 1973, Israel
has had to deal with the threat of a potentially broader Arab
coalition whose forces are undergoing significant expansion and
modernization, subject to virtually no financial constraints.[4]
The response, in terms of order-of-battle, has been: (1) a sizable
increase in Israeli forces, especially in forces-in-being (permanent army, conscripts, and reservists on duty), to the point
where these now comprise over one-fifth of the male Jewish
population in the eighteen to fifty-four age group;[5] and (2)
equipment intensification through the acquisition of more
sophisticated and expensive armaments in ever greater quantities. According to most conventional indicators, Israel has
thereby managed to maintain a reasonable balance against a
variety of potential Arab coalitions and even to improve somewhat its strategic position, especially if Egypt is excluded from
the Arab side of the calculation.

But the cost has been truly staggering. Direct defense outlays
experienced a quantum leap, averaging over 30 percent of GNP
in the period 1974–1980. Indirect costs, including the opportunity costs of resources diverted from civilian production and the
growing burden of servicing a foreign debt amounting to over
$20 billion by the end of 1980, increased as well.[6] The most
obvious consequence of a defense burden of this magnitude has
been that per capita economic growth, in real terms, has virtually ceased since 1974, with doubtful prospects for its resumption unless new resources are found for investment.[7] But with-

out renewed economic growth and some solution to the problem of manpower constraints, even the maximum utilization of national resources, including current territorial assets, may well become an increasingly inadequate response to the security threats confronting Israel.

The costs of a double-track strategy

Despite the obvious difficulties of relying primarily on a strategy of capacity maximization, there are nevertheless grave doubts in Israel as to whether a double-track approach, which almost certainly entails territorial withdrawal, can be safely adopted on the northern and eastern fronts. Even with respect to the peace treaty with Egypt, there were (and are) serious reservations about the advisability of the fundamental exchange — withdrawal from the Sinai in return for security arrangements, political recognition, and normal relations. In the end, the compensations (mostly intangible and reversible) were still felt to outweigh the tangible concessions, and Israel concluded that the overall strategic value of the agreement was positive. But there is widespread conviction in Israel that the same conclusion would not be warranted elsewhere, because the territory at issue is simply too vital to be ceded. Both the Golan Heights (a separate though related problem) and the West Bank and Gaza are felt to be such crucial geomilitary assets that no political agreements or security arrangements can compensate for their loss.

The West Bank and Gaza, of course, are also central to the future evolution of the Palestinian issue, but their loss, particularly the loss of the West Bank, could constitute a danger for Israel regardless of their ultimate *political* disposition. Given the physical characteristics of the West Bank, cession of that territory would complicate by several orders of magnitude the task of defending Israel's vital core area — the narrow coastal plain between Rehovot and Haifa, in which over 60 percent of its population and 80 percent of its industry are concentrated.

The West Bank (Map IV), as delineated by the Israel-Jordan

THE WEST BANK

MAP IV

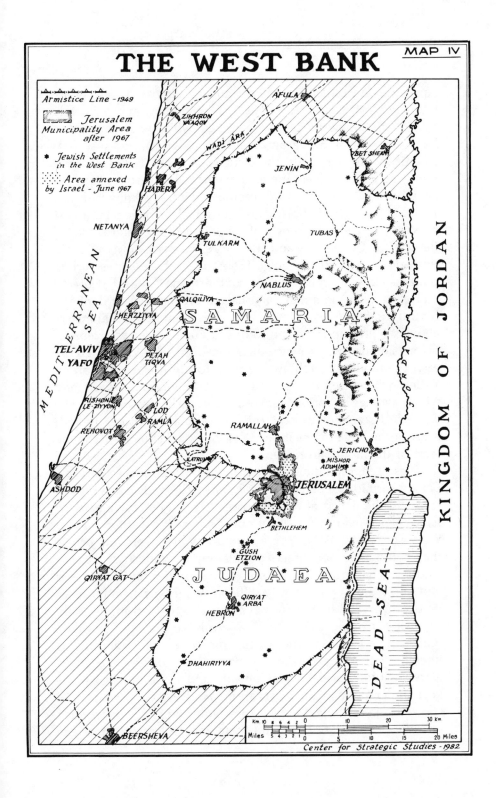

Armistice Line - 1949

Jerusalem Municipality Area after 1967

Jewish Settlements in the West Bank

Area annexed by Israel - June 1967

AFULA

ZIKHRON YAAQOV

WADI ARA

BET SHEAN

JENIN

HADERA

NETANYA

TULKARM

TUBAS

QALQILIYA

NABLUS

SAMARIA

HERZLIYYA

TEL-AVIV YAFO

PETAH TIQVA

MEDITERRANEAN SEA

RISHON LE-ZIYYON

LOD

RAMLA

REHOVOT

RAMALLAH

JERICHO

ASHDOD

LATRUN

MISHOR ADUMIM

JERUSALEM

BETHLEHEM

GUSH ETZION

QIRYAT GAT

JUDAEA

QIRYAT ARBA'

HEBRON

DHAHIRIYYA

KINGDOM OF JORDAN

JORDAN

DEAD SEA

BEERSHEVA

Km. 10 8 6 4 2 0   10   20   30 Km.

Miles 5 4 3 2 1 0   5   10   15   20 Miles

Center for Strategic Studies - 1982

Armistice Agreement of 1949, covers almost 5,600 square kilometers of east-central Palestine, including approximately 100 square kilometers of East Jerusalem which were annexed to Israel in June 1967. From Jenin in the north to just past Dhahiriyya in the south, the distance is about 130 kilometers. From the Jordan River, the area extends westward for approximately 50 kilometers; its westernmost point — Qalqiliya — is just 14 kilometers from the Mediterranean. The region is almost bisected by a small wedge of Israeli territory — the so-called "Jerusalem Corridor" — and therefore consists of two main subregions, a northern bulge (Samaria), whose largest urban center is Nablus, and a smaller, southern one (Judaea), centered on Hebron. The dominant physical feature of the West Bank is a central mountainous spine, which rises from about 500 meters above sea level in the north to over 1,000 meters near Hebron, before sloping away toward the Arad-Beersheba Valley. To the east, the mountains fall away precipitously toward the Jordan Valley, which itself ranges from 1 to 11 kilometers in width and whose average elevation is some 300 meters below sea level. The western descent toward the the coastal plain is more gradual. Most of the large towns in the West Bank are situated along the crest of the mountain ridge.

These geographic and topographic features make the West Bank a formidable defensive asset in Israeli hands and a critical threat in the hands of hostile forces.[8] It is a defensive asset to Israel, when held by Israeli troops, because it constitutes a major obstacle that Arab forces would have to overcome before they could approach Israel's population and industrial concentrations. The Jordan River itself, especially during the summer and fall, is not a particularly difficult water barrier in terms of its depth or width, but it is a much shorter and more easily defensible frontier than the 1949 armistice line (the so-called "Green Line"). During the winter, moreover, there are only a limited number of points at which heavy armor can be brought across without bridging equipment, and these points can be kept under permanent observation. And even if Arab forces succeeded in crossing the river, they would still have to debouch into the open valley floor and there engage Israeli formations enjoying the advantages of prepared fields of fire from topo-graphically superior positions. Further advances would require movement up a very steep gradient on a small number of axes; because of the terrain on the eastern slopes of the Samarian hills, off-road movement is very difficult for mechanized forces. Thus, any assault by Arab ground forces would entail ex-tremely high costs even before they reached the mountain ridge and were able to pose a direct threat to Israel itself, and the physical obstacle confronting this assault would provide time and space for mobilization and application of Israeli counterforce.

Furthermore, control of the West Bank enables Israel to maintain airborne and ground-based observation and electronic information-gathering facilities and surface-to-air missiles — all this 50 kilometers east of the Green Line and, in the case of ground-stations, on highly favorable terrain — thus enhancing its early-warning and antiaircraft capabilities. The West Bank also provides a major training area for the Israel Defense Forces. West Bank airspace is relied on extensively by the Israel Air Force for low-level navigation and night flying exercises and weapons training. Ground space is used to maintain training bases and carry out combined arms exercises. Because of the Israeli withdrawal from Sinai, training space has become a scarce resource.

Finally, control of the West Bank is a major asset in dealing with the problem of terrorism. The maintenance, in situ, of a comprehensive security apparatus — electronic barriers, in-telligence, police, courts, and prisons — enhances Israel's ability to frustrate sabotage operations by breaking up networks, often in their formative stages, and intercepting the flow of sabotage materials into the area.

Taken together, these advantages constitute a formidable defensive asset of which Israel would be deprived if it withdrew from the West Bank, even if the area remained completely demilitarized. Without a significant Israeli military presence in the West Bank, its counterterror capabilities would be seriously impaired, and its response to an Arab military initiative, even if the start-line were still the Jordan River, would be slower, logistically and operationally more demanding, and much more costly.

A situation that permitted the maintenance of military equipment and politically hostile forces in the West Bank itself would dramatically increase the danger. In a worst-case scenario, Arab forces, with the benefit of concentration and surprise, could move from the western Samarian foothills against Israel's narrow waist between Herzliyya and Netanya and, by covering the 15–20 kilometers to the sea, cut Israel in two. Alternatively or simultaneously, they might be able to pinch off the Jerusalem Corridor and isolate Jerusalem. In an effort to deal with such contingencies, Israel would be forced to maintain very large forces-in-being in order to minimize the effect of surprise and reduce the reliance on reserve forces, whose mobilization would be severely complicated by the fact that virtually the whole of the coastal plain is within artillery range of forward West Bank locations. Not only population and industrial centers would be vulnerable to ground fire. Emergency stores, command-and-control centers, and transportation and communications links could be exposed to suppressive fire. Also, most air bases, including the international airport at Lod, could be rendered inoperable by artillery or missile fire. A settlement that permitted an Arab regime to maintain substantial military forces — its own and/or those of foreign states — in the West Bank would pose an intolerable threat to Israel's basic capacity for reactive or anticipatory defense.

Even in a nonwar scenario, saboteurs could take advantage of the longer and more porous border and the knowledge of Israeli territory and the Hebrew language that West Bank residents have acquired since 1967 to gain access to critical targets. A few easily concealed shoulder-fired missiles, for example, could disrupt Israel's international air links. It is possible that cooperation by Arab authorities in dealing with such threats, even if good intentions are assumed, would be an inadequate substitute for Israeli presence.

As a geomilitary asset, the Gaza Strip (Map V) is clearly less vital than the West Bank. A flat, rectangular-shaped stretch of coastal plain about 40 kilometers long and from 5 to 12 kilo-

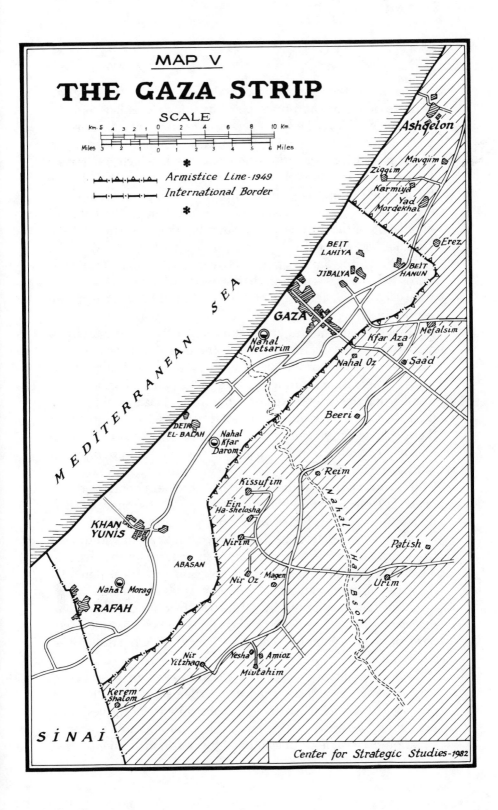

MAP V

THE GAZA STRIP

SCALE

km. 5 4 3 2 1 0 2 4 6 8 10 Km.

Miles 3 2 1 0 1 2 3 4 5 6 Miles

❋

△·△·△·△·△ Armistice Line · 1949

⊢·⊣·⊢·⊣·⊢ International Border

❋

MEDITERRANEAN SEA

Ashqelon

Mavqiim

Ziqqim

Karmiya

Yad Mordekhai

Erez

BEIT LAHIYA

JIBALYA

BEIT HANUN

GAZA

Nahal Netsarim

Kfar Aza

Mefalsim

Nahal Oz

Saad

Beeri

DEIR EL-BALAH

Nahal Kfar Darom

Reim

Kissufim

Nahal Ha Bsor

Ein Ha-shelosha

KHAN YUNIS

Nirim

Patish

ABASAN

Nir Oz

Magen

Urim

Nahal Morag

RAFAH

Nir Yitzhaq

Yesha

Amioz

Mivtahim

Kerem Shalom

SINAI

Center for Strategic Studies · 1982

meters wide, the Gaza Strip contains no natural fortifications and provides no real topographic advantage to either defender or attacker. Nevertheless, an Israeli military presence in the Strip makes it more difficult for any potential attacker to develop an offensive along the coast road, which has served throughout history as the main axis of advance into Palestine for invaders from the south. Withdrawal from the area would entail moving Israeli forward defense lines along the coast 40 kilometers to the northeast, but since Egypt is prevented by the Egyptian-Israeli peace treaty from deploying troops in the eastern third of Sinai, or heavy weapons in the eastern two-thirds (Map VI), such a withdrawal would not increase the proximity to Israeli territory of the major military force in the region (as long as Egypt adhered to the peace agreement). However, even a non-Egyptian administration could establish a modest regular military force, and there are Israeli targets, including some important installations in the Ashkelon area, within conventional artillery range of the Strip. Furthermore, dismantling the Israeli security apparatus in Gaza would greatly increase the technical capacity of terrorists to operate from there, particularly given the availability of a coastline which either dissidents or a hostile regime could use to bring in sabotage materials.[9]

In short, control of the West Bank and Gaza confers advantages on Israel that would certainly be lost if it withdrew; their utilization by Arab forces represents yet further danger. Two calculations will determine the net effect on Israel of withdrawal from these areas: the extent to which substitutes for the absolute advantages can be found, and the probability that the potential dangers will be actualized. Technology plays some role in the first, but both are primarily a function of politics—the actual provisions of any settlement and, most important, the long-term political dynamics that a settlement would be likely to stimulate.

If the pursuit of a double-track strategy is to recommend itself to Israel, its object — a political settlement — must therefore promise to create a matrix of constraints, incentives, and political dynamics in the region resulting in a national security situation preferable to that implied by continuing reliance on a

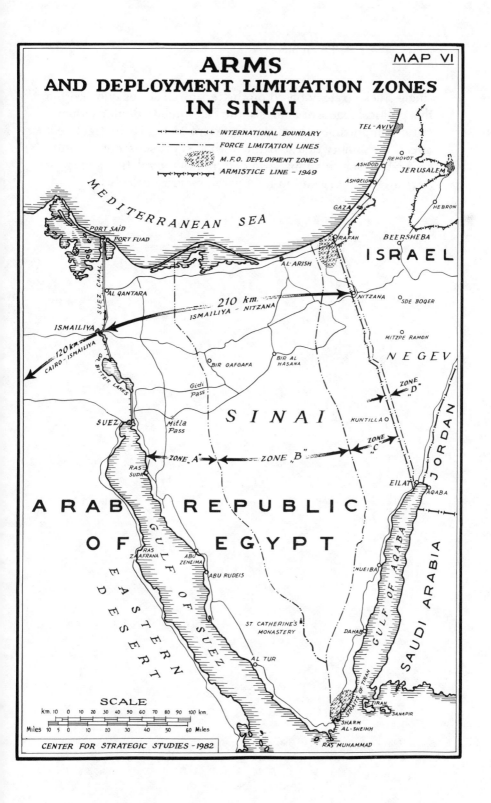

ARMS
AND DEPLOYMENT LIMITATION ZONES
IN SINAI

MAP VI

- INTERNATIONAL BOUNDARY
- FORCE LIMITATION LINES
- M.F.O. DEPLOYMENT ZONES
- ARMISTICE LINE – 1949

MEDITERRANEAN SEA

TEL-AVIV
REHOVOT
ASHDOD
JERUSALEM
ASHQELON
HEBRON
GAZA
RAFAH
BEERSHEBA

ISRAEL

PORT SAID
PORT FUAD
AL-ARISH
AL QANTARA
NITZANA
SDE BOQER

210 km.
ISMAILIYA – NITZANA

MITZPE RAMON

ISMAILIYA
120 km.
CAIRO-ISMAILIYA

BITTER LAKES

BIR GAFGAFA
BIR AL HASANA

NEGEV

Gidi Pass

ZONE "D"

SINAI

KUNTILLA

ZONE "A"
ZONE "B"
ZONE "C"

SUEZ
Mitla Pass

JORDAN

RAS SUDR
EILAT
AQABA

ARAB REPUBLIC

OF EGYPT

RAS Z. AFRANA
ABU ZENEIMA

ABU RUDEIS
NUEIBA

EASTERN

DESERT

ST CATHERINE'S MONASTERY
DAHAB

AL TUR

SHARM AL-SHEIKH
RAS MUHAMMAD

GULF OF SUEZ
GULF OF AQABA
STRAITS OF TIRAN
TIRAN
SANAFIR

SAUDI ARABIA

SCALE
km. 10 0 10 20 30 40 50 60 70 80 90 100 km.
Miles 10 5 0   10   20   30   40   50   60 Miles

CENTER FOR STRATEGIC STUDIES - 1982

single-track strategy based on the territorial status quo. Within this political frame of analysis, the Palestinian question assumes critical importance, because the extent to which its treatment affects the quality of a settlement, that is, the subsequent nature of Arab-Israeli relations, also determines the relative impact of territorial withdrawal on the overall security calculus.

3

Implications of Alternatives
to a Palestinian State

The advisability to Israel of a settlement involving the creation of an independent Palestinian state can be properly assessed only on the basis of a comparative analysis of possible alternative outcomes. Such an analysis requires some consideration of the probable risks/costs and benefits of those alternatives.

The alternatives can be roughly classified into five principal model-types: (1) nonsettlement of the Israeli-Arab conflict (with or without Israeli withdrawal); (2) "territorial compromise"; (3) nonterritorial settlements, that is, various forms of functional partition; (4) an Israeli-Palestinian territorial settlement that bypasses the PLO; and, (5) an Israeli-Arab territorial settlement that bypasses any Palestinian interlocutor. Of these possible outcomes, only the first can be secured by unilateral Israeli action. The others require Arab partners, and they are therefore not all equally attainable. For purposes of this study, however, the projected long-term strategic impact on Israel of the various outcomes is the most significant consideration in judging their advisability.

Nonsettlement

The first model-type refers to two conceptual extremes: perpetuation of the status quo and unilateral Israeli withdrawal from the West Bank and Gaza Strip.

In the absence of any political settlement, Israel could continue to hold all the territories under its control after the completion of the withdrawal from Sinai. The geomilitary value of these territories is very high, but their overall strategic value must be assessed within a broader national security context that addresses both the general political consequences of perpetuation of the territorial status quo and the specific costs of continued Israeli rule in the West Bank and Gaza.

With respect to the general consequences of the status quo, the fundamental point to be stressed is that it is incompatible with peace. Important differences exist within the Arab world over a number of questions — the acceptability of peace under any circumstances, the requisite territorial and other features of a peace agreement, the urgency of and format for a solution of the Palestinian problem — but the lowest common denominator in the Arab consensus is the demand for Israeli withdrawal from the territories taken in 1967. Consequently, Israeli withdrawal may not be a sufficient condition for peace, but it is clearly a necessary one, and continued Israeli control of the West Bank and Gaza, barring some highly improbable reversal of Arab policy, means a continuation of the state-of-war. But a perpetuation of the territorial status quo does not also mean a perpetuation of the strategic status quo. Neither the political constellation — regional and international — nor the balance of forces is likely to remain constant.

Perhaps the most critical strategic implication of the territorial status quo is the danger that it will lead to the emergence of broader and more effective Arab war coalitions, with which Israel, because of its resource limitations, will be increasingly hard-pressed to cope. Since 1973, the Arab world as a whole, because of its immense petro-dollar revenues, has been freed of virtually all the political and financial constraints that previously affected its ability to exploit its manpower potential. The result has been an impressive buildup in the order-of-battle of several Arab states. Particularly large increases have been registered in the armed forces of Iraq, Saudi Arabia, and Libya, and in the armor and aircraft inventories of these countries and Syria as well. Jordanian forces, while experiencing more modest growth, have undergone a marked qualitative improvement in terms of mobility and equipment modernization.[1]

It is not, however, the separate capabilities of individual Arab states, but rather the power of an expanded and properly coordinated Arab war coalition that represents a potentially mortal threat to Israel's security. The obstacles in the path of effective Arab military coordination are enormous. Because of mutual suspicions, competing aspirations, different regime-types, and historical rivalries, it is difficult for the Arab states to agree on a common political basis for a war plan. Front-line states are reluctant to permit the long-term stationing of foreign Arab armies on their territory. And although some degree of weapons compatibility has always existed, as it does now between Iraq and Syria and between Jordan and Saudi Arabia, nonstandard equipment inventories and tables of organization seriously complicate all-Arab interoperability. For these reasons, effective coordination has eluded the Arabs thus far. Nevertheless, the specter of a functioning united Arab command, even if limited in scope, has always haunted Israeli military planners. The activation of an operational command post in Amman in May 1967, within the framework of the United Arab Command, was one factor that compelled Israel to preempt, before its potential value to the Arabs could be realized. The Syrian-Egyptian coalition in 1973, though institutionally more modest, was able to overcome some of the inherent limitations on Arab cooperation and to produce a simultaneous initiative on two fronts; the fact that Syrian-Egyptian coordination later broke down does not negate the significance of the initial success. Indeed, the Syrian-Egyptian attack in 1973 demonstrates that future Arab coalitions need not be conditional on the achievement of political integration or even a permanent military alliance. An ad hoc joint planning and operations staff, for a limited period, might suffice to launch a coordinated assault and place intolerable strains on Israel.

Israeli retention of the occupied territories, including the West Bank, acts as an additional impetus for the Arab states to overcome the obstacles to military coordination, even as it imperils the political legitimacy of Israeli preemption (regardless of the military necessity). As a factor in the Middle East state system, it is a symbol of Israel's superior military status, and is perceived by some Arab states as tangible evidence of their suspicion that Israel, whatever its conscious intentions, is an inherently expansionist entity, hence, a direct danger to them. The consequence of such regional dynamics, historically, has been an almost reflexive attempt to restore balance through combination.

In addition to this "systemic" consideration, Israeli control of the West Bank and Gaza also constitutes an ideological-political prod to Arab action. By serving as a constant reminder of the unresolved Palestinian question, the occupation minimizes the ability of Arab states to reach an accommodation with Israel or even, in the current circumstances, to assume a posture of indifference. It is in this sense that the centrality of the Palestinian question to Israeli security must be understood.

Since 1948, Palestinian-Arab relations have been marked by contradiction. On the one hand, Palestinians have been treated in Arab countries as foreigners, and their reception has ranged from disinterest to outright hostility. Even in Jordan, where official distinctions were virtually eliminated and integration has been most pronounced, a sense of separate identity nevertheless persists. Indeed, the experiences of most Palestinians in Arab countries, even outside the refugee camps, have tended, if anything, to reinforce their particularistic national consciousness.[2]

On the other hand, the "cause" of Palestine has elicited near-universal sympathy and support in the Arab world. For many, both inside and outside of government, the "loss" of Palestine represents the last and most visible symbol of "western domination" elsewhere eradicated from the Middle East and thus a continuing provocation of the Arab world as a whole. Furthermore, Israeli control of Jerusalem is perceived as an affront to Muslim religious sensitivities, even, though to a lesser extent, among non-Arab Muslims. Solidarity with the Palestinian cause therefore provides much of the cement for what remains of the sense of Arab unity.[3] And states that aspire to leadership within the Arab world must therefore play an active role in support of this cause.

In addition to the emotional impulse for a solution to the

Palestinian problem, there are some distinctly practical motives at work as well. Wherever there are large concentrations of Palestinians — in the oil-producing states (especially Kuwait), in Lebanon, Jordan, and to some extent in Syria — they represent sources of domestic political instability. Because of their social marginality, their highly developed political consciousness, and their lack of collective vested interest in the established order, they are often viewed as unreliable and irresponsible, producers and consumers of radicalism on their own and potential catalysts of indigenous discontent as well. Various regimes and social formations, ranging from privileged classes in the Gulf to Shi'a groups in Lebanon, therefore seek, in a solution of the Palestine problem, some relief from their own immediate dilemmas.[4] Even among Israel's most "natural" allies in the region — the Maronite Christians of Lebanon — there is a feeling that the establishment of a Palestinian state would justify the removal from Lebanon of the greatest irritant (in their view) to their country's body politic.[5]

For these reasons, continued nonsettlement increases the probability that a systematically and ideologically inspired Arab war coalition will emerge, at least on the Eastern Front. And most dangerous of all, from Israel's perspective, is the possibility that confrontation could be renewed on the Western Front as well. For as long as there is no solution of the Palestinian problem, or at least progress toward a solution, the peace between Israel and Egypt must remain fragile and tenuous. Despite the Israeli preference to separate the two issues, there is a clear political linkage.[6] From the beginning of the peace process, President Sadat emphasized that he sought, not a separate Egyptian-Israeli peace, but a comprehensive settlement, based on Israeli withdrawal and recognition of the Palestinians' right to establish an independent state if they so desired.[7] Both the Camp David Accords and the Egyptian-Israeli Peace Treaty which those Accords ultimately spawned made explicit provision for a settlement that took account of "the legitimate rights of the Palestinian people."[8] But even more critical than the sincerity of Sadat's peaceful intentions, particularly in view of his assassination, are the dynamic implications for Egypt of nonsettlement.

Egypt paid a heavy cost, in lives and treasure, for its thirty-year-long confrontation with Israel. Peace promises to alleviate these costs and to provide some significant benefits as well, especially in the form of American economic and military assistance. A casual reversal of course would jeopardize these achievements and is therefore not very probable. Nevertheless, the peace treaty with Israel also involves a major cost for Egypt — a large measure of political, economic, and cultural isolation within the Arab world. This cost is tolerable, as a temporary burden. But Egyptians were told that Sadat's initiative would set in motion a process to which other Arabs would eventually adhere. They are unlikely to accept isolation from their cultural hinterland and the loss of Egypt's role as the natural leader of the Arab world on a permanent basis. Even in the early post-treaty era, there were signs of disillusionment within the Egyptian elite,[9] and in the absence of further progress, the conviction that Egypt is paying an inordinate price for Israel's Palestinian policy will probably grow. If, under such circumstances, tensions in the region were to escalate, then Arab inducements to Egypt to resume its position at the head of an Arab coalition would be difficult to resist. At the very least, perpetuation of the status quo provides Egyptian opponents of the peace and/or of the regime with an important lever in their domestic struggle. Retention of the West Bank and Gaza therefore increases the probability of a collapse of the peace treaty with Egypt and the emergence of a broader Arab coalition, with the consequent loss of political maneuverability and the ultimate threat to Israel of a two-front war. And whether or not such a coalition actually materializes, Israel will have to take the danger into account in its military planning, meaning additional demands on economic and manpower resources already stretched very thin.

Thus, retention of the West Bank and Gaza constitutes a fundamental political-strategic risk for Israel because it encourages the expansion or consolidation of an Arab war coalition, undermines the strategic benefits of the peace with Egypt, and perpetuates or exacerbates the burden of coping with these security threats. But in addition to this basic risk, there are a number of more proximate costs attached to Israel's continuing rule in the West Bank and Gaza.

The most immediate of these has been the intensification of explicitly Palestinian consciousness and of hostility between the Palestinians and Israel. Because of the cultural affinity of the Arab ruling authorities (Egyptian in the Gaza Strip and, especially, Jordanian in the West Bank), the regime before 1967 was not perceived as unequivocally "foreign," and it was there-fore possible for the ruled to tolerate some ambiguity in their own collective identity. But since 1967, the Israeli regime in these territories has been alien to the Arab residents in every imaginable respect, and with the sharpening of the dichotomy between rulers and ruled and the exclusion by Israel of com-peting foci of political loyalty, the crystallization of a distinct Palestinian identity in these territories. with a clear anti-Israel essence, has been undeniable.

In many cases, Israeli officers and local Palestinian officials have managed to maintain correct, if not warm, working rela-tionships. Economic ties have also grown up between Jews and Arabs, and in a few cases, even personal friendships have been established or reestablished. Nevertheless, the basic relationship has remained that of military occupation. The day-to-day qual-ity of this relationship fluctuates in response to specific events (both inside and outside the territories), but its fundamental character — the monopolization of power by one national entity and the collective powerlessness of the other — makes tension and mutual suspicion unavoidable. Under such circumstances, even ordinary civic issues are quickly suffused with nationalist overtones and become subjects, not of civic politics, but of Israeli-Palestinian confrontation. Thus, attempts to impose on the territories the value-added tax (VAT) adopted in Israel led to violent demonstrations in the West Bank in 1976 and to a general strike in the Gaza Strip in 1981, and political figures in both areas quickly attempted to escalate the issue into general resistance to the occupation. In January 1980 an Israeli declara-tion of intent to take over the concession of the Arab-owned Jerusalem District Electricity Company provoked widespread protests against the threat to the "Arab character" of the enterprise. And a work-action at the end of 1980 by government-employed teachers in the West Bank, protesting their low wage levels compared to those of Israeli teachers, ultimately resulted in calls for a general strike and in some stone-throwing incidents, as well as a barely submerged clash between Jordan and the PLO over handling of the issue.[10]

The politicization of essentially civic issues is an inevitable by-product of the collective inequality inherent in occupation. Measures by Israel that seem to portend the perpetuation of the situation (land requisition, establishment of settlements, imposition of a civilian administration) further provoke Palestinian sensibilities. The result is permanent discontent, which is periodically expressed in stoning of or firing on Israeli vehicles, and in strikes, demonstrations, and other disruptions, often by secondary-school and college students whose political awareness is high and whose direct material stake in tranquility is minimal.

Such disturbances, though sometimes bloody, are far from being the civil revolt frequently portrayed in the media, and they have not seriously challenged Israel's ability to remain in control. Nor are they likely to do so in the future. Given the territories' compactness, the pervasiveness and effectiveness of the Israeli security network, the fear of Israeli counterviolence or deportations, and the vested interest of important social forces — workers as well as bourgeoisie — in domestic peace, the probability of a widespread and sustained uprising is quite low, at least in the absence of much more provocative Israeli actions or the outbreak of protracted military conflict on the Eastern Front. Relative tranquility therefore prevails most of the time, but whatever coexistence there is results from the Israeli monopoly of force, rather than from any psychopolitical reconciliation between Israelis and Palestinians.

Nevertheless, the continuing effort to maintain or restore law and order has itself had a perceptible, if immeasurable, impact on Israel's moral self-assurance and national cohesion — an important element in its ability to overcome material inferiority. Israelis, by now, are familiar with the image of troops patrolling Arab streets; they have been exposed to the even more unedifying spectacle of Israeli soldiers containing or dispersing crowds of schoolchildren, sometimes with measures that result in physical injury, or death. Many view the occupation-related functions of the Israel Defense Forces as a deviation from their role as defender of the nation's independence, and thus a danger to their traditional ethos. Cases of repugnant behavior in the territories, or, conversely, of conscientious refusal by soldiers to serve there, although rare, are evidence of the kind of moral dangers that prolonged occupation may pose.

A source of even greater concern are the emerging doubts about the fundamental direction of Israel's present course and the kind of society it implies.[11] In its vision of collective emancipation and normalization in Eretz Yisrael of the Jewish national condition, Zionism aspired to self-rule, not to rule over others. If this aspiration contradicted Arab aspirations and ultimately produced Jewish rule over Arabs, that was partly the result of ignorance and partly of an unfortunate and unintended historical process, determined, in Israeli eyes, by Arab intransigence rather than by Jewish malice. The fact remains, however, that Israel finds itself frustrating the Palestinian desire for collective self-expression, and many Israelis are beset by doubts whether what is necessary as a temporary security measure is also justifiable as a long-term political relationship.

These doubts are likely to grow if current demographic trends continue and the Arab population under Israeli rule or control approaches, matches, and ultimately surpasses the Jewish population. The direction and rate of change in the population balance is determined by a number of factors, but the most volatile, and vital, component is net Jewish immigration, and there is reason to believe that this variable is itself affected adversely (from the Israeli perspective) by the state-of-war implied by the Israeli rule in the West Bank and Gaza. For aside from its economic consequences, the occupation also stimulates a certain hardening of public life in Israel and encourages the emergence of a political culture that may provoke some Israelis to emigrate and alienate non-Israeli Jews, including potential immigrants, most of whom by now are found in countries where liberalism, secularism, and tolerance are the prevailing social norms.[12]

Demography is a powerful disincentive to formal absorption of the West Bank and Gaza. Such a measure would confront Israel with a cruel dilemma: to exclude the Palestinian population from the political system, thus undermining Israeli democracy, or to incorporate it, thereby diminishing the Jewish character of the state. Incorporation also raises a different risk to democracy, namely, that normal political divisions among Jews would be suppressed in order to avoid governmental dependence on, and disproportionate influence for, Arab representatives in parliament. But even perpetuation of the territories' undefined status represents a threat to another value — the rehabilitation of the Jewish social structure — which is central to Labor Zionism and implicit, to some extent, in the broader Zionist aspiration to a normal national existence. For as workers from the territories moved into the Israeli economy after 1967 — mostly as unskilled day laborers — they began to form an ethnically distinct underclass.[13] Such a phenomenon is not atypical of contact elsewhere between technologically advanced and developing societies. Nor does it necessarily represent, despite the concentration of Palestinian workers in the construction, agriculture, and service sectors, an irreversible and potentially dangerous Israeli dependence on "foreign" workers. Many of the positions they fill may be eliminated by advanced production techniques. Nevertheless, as long as this phenomenon persists, it is, for some Israelis, ethically uncomfortable — both as a distortion of their vision of Israeli society and as a symptom of the broader Israeli-Palestinian relationship.

Finally, Israeli control of the territories, hence of the Palestinian population, entails a high cost in the international arena. Israel's inclinations to claim these territories, for security and especially for historical-ideological reasons, have aroused virtually unanimous opposition. This was evident immediately after 1967, simply because the acquisition of territory by war was viewed as inadmissible. It has become more pronounced over time, as the Palestinian dimension of the Arab-Israeli conflict has become more salient and Palestinian demands have gained increasing, albeit conditional, recognition. International support for the Palestinian national movement does not, to be sure, derive solely from a moral imperative. Considerations of oil, Arab markets, and the desirability of strategic access to the Middle East play important roles, especially for those states not otherwise attached to Arab, Muslim, or Third-World causes. Nevertheless, these considerations have combined with — and probably contributed to — a growing international consensus on the legitimacy of Palestinian claims, especially the claim to self-determination and an independent state. Against these claims, Israel has waged a futile and increasingly lonely diplomatic campaign that appears to clash with both the practical interests of third parties and the dominant political idea of the modern era.

The United States, because of its position as a global super-power, and for domestic political reasons as well, has adopted a decidedly less commercial approach to the Arab-Israeli conflict than have other third parties. As a result, the most critical foreign actor, from Israel's perspective, has also been the most reluctant to endorse Arab claims. Nevertheless, it is clear that even American attitudes toward the acceptability of the status quo diverge quite sharply from those of Israel. The American position with respect to the territorial issue, first articulated in 1969 and consistently upheld ever since, is that "any changes in the pre-existing lines should not reflect the weight of conquest and should be confined to insubstantial alterations required for mutual security."[14] In response to intimations by the Likud government in 1978 that evacuation of the Sinai satisfied the "withdrawal of Israeli armed forces from territories occupied" provision of United Nations Security Council Resolution 242, Secretary of State Cyrus Vance declared that the resolution applies "to all fronts, and — more specifically — to the West Bank and Gaza."[15] There is no reason to assume that the American position on the territorial issue will become more sympathetic to Israeli claims.

On the issue of Palestinian national aspirations, the United States has been much more noncommittal. In general, however, there has been increasing sensitivity to the Palestinian question as it has grown in international saliency, and particularly as its resolution has been perceived as a prerequisite to the successful pursuit of other US interests in the region, especially improved US-Saudi relations. Although the United States has thus far officially rejected an independent Palestinian state as the basis of a settlement, there have been signs of growing receptivity to the idea.[16] In any event, it is clear that the US position on this issue is instrumental, that is, a function of its place in the broader American approach to the region, and it could therefore change if the cost to the United States of nonsettlement becomes intolerable.

Israeli efforts to perpetuate the status quo therefore not only risk growing international isolation, with consequent damage to Israel's self-confidence and moral unity; they also increase the danger that American — even American Jewish — responsiveness to Israel's military and economic needs will become contingent on Israeli acquiescence in an externally devised settlement, possibly less satisfactory than one that Israel might secure through its own efforts.

In sum, retention of the West Bank and Gaza, especially the former, confers on Israel some important military advantages but also involves national security costs — economic, diplomatic, moral, and demographic — and risks the unraveling of the peace with Egypt and the intensifying hostility of the remainder of the Arab world. These costs are weighty enough to raise serious doubts about Israel's long-term ability to pursue its traditional strategy of capacity maximization and simultaneously to promote other central values. And aside from a revolutionary change in Arab attitudes or in the balance of international economic and political-military power, these costs can be reduced to more manageable proportions only by a political settlement that unavoidably diminishes the territorial base of Israel's defense capability as well.

A settlement that inspired confidence in its ability to endure would offset the geomilitary value of the West Bank and Gaza Strip sufficiently to recommend it over a strategy of the status quo. A settlement that was, because of its political character, partial or inherently unstable, would not. Neither would any settlement that permitted the introduction into these territories of substantial military forces, no matter how nonhostile those forces might promise to be. In this context, the distinction often made between offensive and defensive capacity is meaningless, since even a "defensive" force in situ, especially in the West Bank, could prevent an Israeli anticipatory forward deployment long enough to permit larger Eastern Front forces to move into the West Bank. Given the short warning-times and narrow margins of error imposed by geography, the presence of a large non-Israeli military force in the West Bank is therefore unacceptable.

Even less advisable would be Israeli withdrawal conditional on no settlement at all. Within the "nonsettlement" rubric, such a measure might be expected to reduce some of the immediate costs associated with Israeli rule in the territories. Nevertheless, the territorial status quo is preferable to partial, unstable, or militarily threatening political settlements and is preferable, a fortiori, to unilateral withdrawal. For in the latter case, Israel would be deprived of all the advantages of control of the territories but would gain none of the political benefits of even a partial settlement, with the exception of some inconsequential propaganda gains and perhaps a very transitory moderation of Arab animosity to Israel.

Some rationale for unconditional withdrawal may have existed immediately after the 1967 war; in light of subsequent developments, the very idea is now so ill-advised that it is imaginable only as an involuntary measure, that is, in response to external pressure. Pressure might conceivably be exerted by the Palestinians themselves, in the form of local resistance that raises to intolerable levels the direct cost to Israel of continued occupation. A more plausible source of pressure, however, is the United States, which might threaten to make continued military and economic assistance contingent on Israeli agreement to evacuate the West Bank and Gaza. Even if the American threat were accompanied by promises of various American security guarantees, the outcome, in the absence of any Israeli-Arab settlement, would be the establishment in Israel of an American protectorate whose durability and credibility would be highly suspect.

Awareness of this defect is likely to deter the United States from attempting, probably without success, to impose a nonsettlement on Israel. A more probable danger, already suggested, is an American effort to engineer an agreement that contains some verbal components of formal peace but lacks many of Israel's diplomatic, military, spatial, and temporal risk-minimization requirements. Such an agreement might ostensibly be mutually acceptable, but both its substance and the process by which it was achieved would inevitably impart to it an imposed character, thereby eliminating a vital element of psychological rapprochement and stimulating Arab hopes that the effectiveness of direct or indirect pressure on Israel had not yet been exhausted.

A "settlement" of this sort would not be significantly more stable, definitive, or secure than a nonsettlement, and Israel would undoubtedly resist with a tenacity proportional to the nonreciprocal nature of the concessions demanded. For the same reason, the United States may continue to resist the temptation to operate its levers of potential pressure. Nevertheless, American inhibitions against pursuing such an approach may also diminish as the status quo persists and Israeli dependence increases, raising the probability that this outcome will yet materialize, not as a separate (and counterindicated) Israeli policy alternative, but as another undesirable and unforeseen consequence of attempts to perpetuate the status quo.

Territorial compromise

Theoretically, of course, a permanent and comprehensive peace between Israel and the Arab world would completely eliminate the security threat to Israel and render the question of defense capability academic. Perfect, perpetual peace, however, has always been a utopian ideal. There are particularly strong doubts in Israel about ultimate Arab and Palestinian intentions to adhere to a formal peace and about the capacity of the inter-Arab political system to sustain it. Many Israeli decisionmakers and opinion leaders have therefore advocated a "golden mean"—a solution that minimizes the political-demographic liabilities while maximizing Israel's geographic-topographic security assets. In the Israeli political lexicon, "territorial compromise" provides one key to such a solution. The purpose of territorial compromise is to transfer the bulk of the Palestinian population to Jordanian jurisdiction, thus relieving Israel of the burden of direct rule, while allowing it to reserve strategically vital and (coincidentally) thinly settled areas in the West Bank.

The best-known variant of territorial compromise is the so-called "Allon Plan," named after the late Foreign Minister and Deputy Prime Minister Yigal Allon. There is no single standard version of the Allon Plan; Allon himself proposed several slightly different elaborations. The main features of the plan, however, are clear. Israel would retain the Jordan Valley rift and the Judaean Desert, including the easternmost ridge of the Samarian and Judaean mountains, while permitting the political unification with the East Bank of the heavily populated central core of the West Bank. Uninterrupted communications between the two Banks would be ensured by a corridor under Arab sovereignty along the Jericho-Ramallah axis (Map VII). In this way, Israel could continue to benefit from some measure of strategic depth and topographic advantage, while the Palestinians would be free of Israeli rule and could express their political identity in a single Jordanian-Palestinian state.[17]

There are a number of difficulties confronting a settlement based on territorial compromise. For example, no consensus exists within Israel on which territories are essential to provide a minimal "safety-net" in case the settlement breaks down. Many authoritative observers are convinced that Israeli security requires military control of the central mountain ridge, even if this entails retention of the most densely populated areas.[18] Even within the Labor party, which, unlike the Likud, officially endorses the principle of territorial compromise, there is no unanimity on the extent of permissible compromise. Yigal Allon himself sometimes argued that southern Gaza, the Etzion Bloc, and the Judaean Desert up to Kiryat Arba should be included in his plan,[19] and the Labor party platform for the 1981 elections specified that the Etzion Bloc and a Jerusalem Bloc stretching eastward to the Ma'ale Adumim complex, in addition to the Jordan Valley, are indispensable security zones.[20]

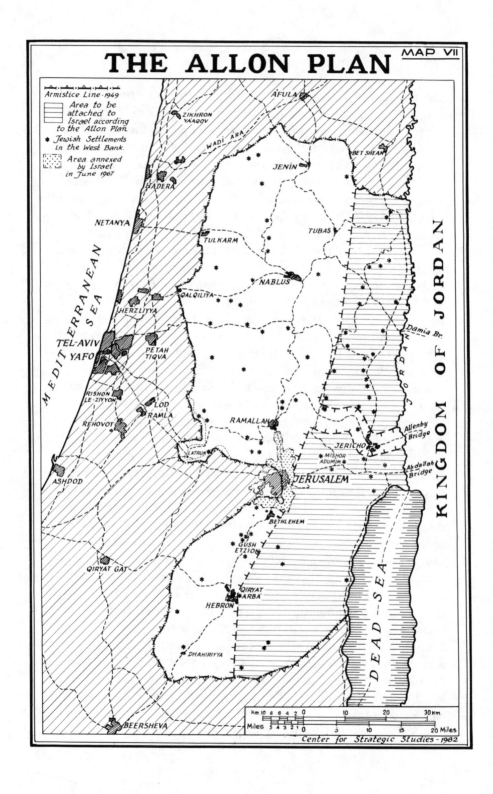

THE ALLON PLAN

MAP VII

Armistice Line · 1949
Area to be attached to Israel according to the Allon Plan.
★ Jewish Settlements in the West Bank.
Area annexed by Israel in June 1967

MEDITERRANEAN SEA

KINGDOM OF JORDAN

DEAD SEA

JORDAN

ZIKHRON YAAQOV
AFULA
BET SHEAN
JENIN
HADERA
NETANYA
TULKARM
TUBAS
NABLUS
HERZLIYYA
QALQILIYA
TEL-AVIV YAFO
PETAH TIQVA
Damia Br.
RISHON LE-ZIYYON
LOD
RAMLA
REHOVOT
RAMALLAH
ASHDOD
LATRUN
Allenby Bridge
JERICHO
MISHOR ADUMIM
Abdallah Bridge
JERUSALEM
BETHLEHEM
GUSH ETZION
QIRYAT GAT
QIRYAT ARBA
HEBRON
DHAHIRIYYA
BEERSHEVA

WADI ARA

Km. 10 8 6 4 2 0   10   20   30 Km.
Miles 5 4 3 2 1 0   5   10   15   20 Miles

Center for Strategic Studies - 1982

The major obstacle to a territorial compromise is political, that is, the extreme improbability of finding any Arab interlocutor with whom to compromise. If there has been any consistency in the Arab approach to a settlement, it has been anchored in the minimal demand for complete Israeli withdrawal from the territories occupied in 1967. For some Arab actors, even this is less than sufficient; for none is it more than sufficient. Every inter-Arab forum, including the Arab Summit Conference held in Baghdad in November 1978 to protest the Camp David Agreements, has posited full withdrawal as a condition for peace.[21] In his speech to the Knesset, Sadat emphasized that total Israeli withdrawal was "a logical and undisputed fact," without which peace and security would be meaningless.[22] Of those Arabs most directly involved, King Husayn has been unwavering in his insistence that peace requires complete Israeli withdrawal from the occupied territories, including East Jerusalem. [23] In addition to his public statements, Husayn has held tenaciously to this position in private encounters over the years with Israeli leaders. In a meeting with Israeli Foreign Minister Moshe Dayan in August 1977, for example, he explained that he could not yield even an inch because an agreement to partition the West Bank would be considered treason.[24] The Palestinians, at least insofar as they are represented by the PLO, have never indicated a willingness to make peace with Israel under any circumstances, so the question of territorial division is officially moot. It should be pointed out, however, that even the whole of the West Bank and Gaza would constitute a far worse territorial compromise, from their perspective, than either the 1937 British Royal Commission recommendation or the 1947 United Nations Partition Plan (Map VIII), both of which they rejected unequivocally. The prospects of Palestinian agreement to peace with Israel, however remote, must therefore be judged as virtually nonexistent if "compromise" means a further reduction of Arab territory, particularly now that the precedent of full withdrawal has been established in the Sinai.

The improbability of a settlement based on any demarcation line other than the Green Line is not, however, based solely on the intensity of Arab declarations. After all, an equally intense

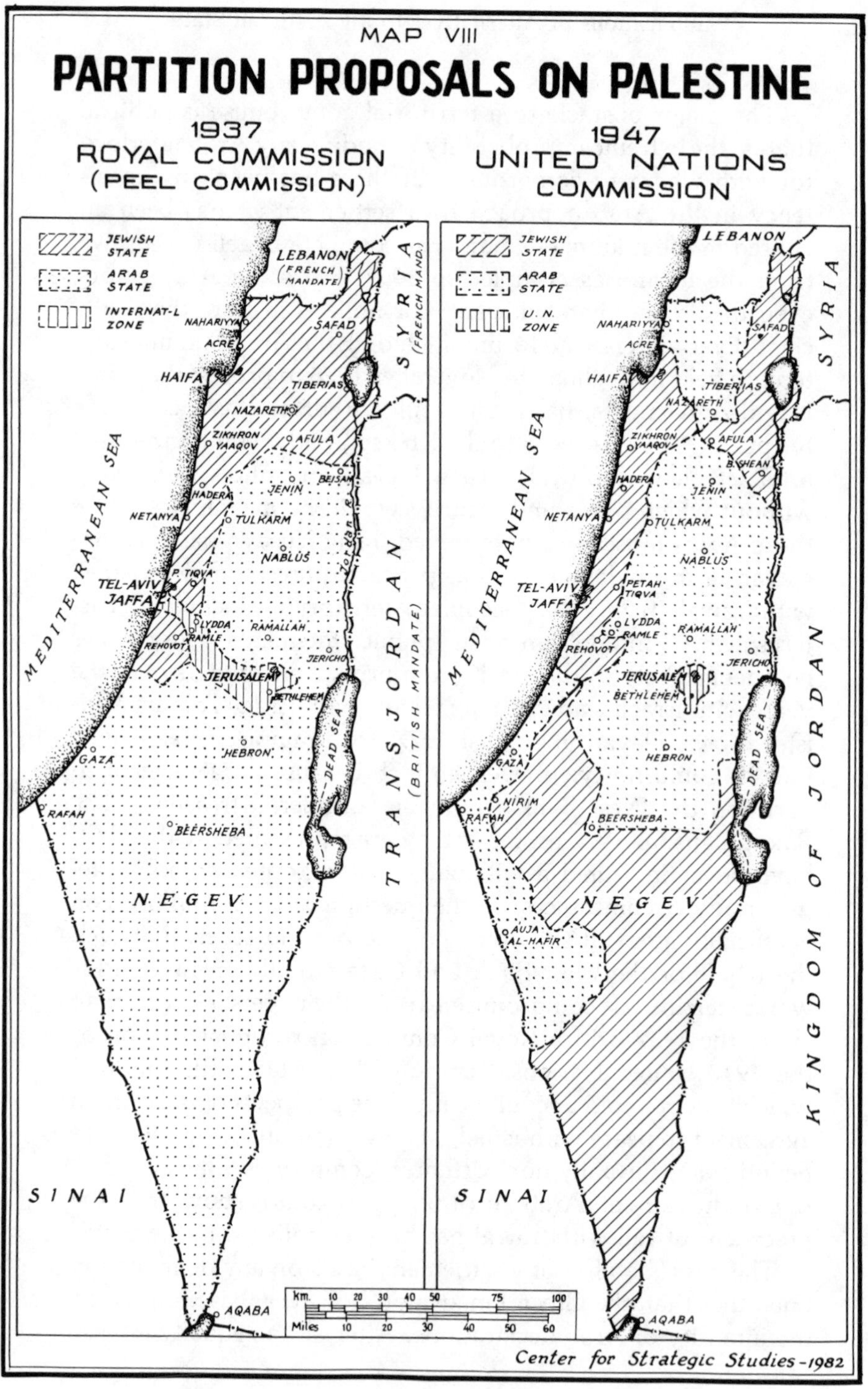
MAP VIII
PARTITION PROPOSALS ON PALESTINE
1937
ROYAL COMMISSION
(PEEL COMMISSION)
1947
UNITED NATIONS
COMMISSION
JEWISH STATE
ARAB STATE
INTERNAT-L ZONE
U.N. ZONE
LEBANON
(FRENCH MANDATE)
SYRIA
(FRENCH MAND.)
NAHARIYYA
ACRE
HAIFA
SAFAD
TIBERIAS
NAZARETH
ZIKHRON YAAQOV
AFULA
BEISAN
B. SHEAN
HADERA
JENIN
NETANYA
TULKARM
NABLUS
P. TIQVA
PETAH TIQVA
TEL-AVIV
JAFFA
LYDDA
RAMLE
REHOVOT
RAMALLAH
JERICHO
JERUSALEM
BETHLEHEM
HEBRON
GAZA
NIRIM
RAFAH
BEERSHEBA
AUJA AL-HAFIR
NEGEV
SINAI
AQABA
MEDITERRANEAN SEA
DEAD SEA
Jordan R.
TRANSJORDAN
(BRITISH MANDATE)
KINGDOM OF JORDAN
Km. 10 20 30 40 50 75 100
Miles 10 20 30 40 50 60
Center for Strategic Studies - 1982

Israeli determination *not* to retreat to the Green Line could easily be documented. The inevitability of the Green Line derives mostly from the logic of the situation, that is, from its unique salience. A bargaining situation is a problem of coordination, the solution of which is almost invariably a reflection of its own conspicuousness or unique prominence. In the absence of some self-evident "natural" (that is, physical or demographic) solution, prominence depends on a more capricious factor — analogy, precedent, accidental arrangement, symmetry, or aesthetic or geometric configuration.[25]

The Green Line was, for almost twenty years, a de facto border (and is still, in some sense, a border even today), and it commands a large measure of international consensus. It is thus the only line in Palestine that displays the prominence, the innate magnetism, to achieve convergence. In other such conflicts, it seems "that a cynic could have predicted the outcome on the basis of some 'obvious' focus for agreement, some strong suggestion contained in the situation itself, without much regard to the merits of the case, the arguments to be made, or the pressures to be applied during the bargaining. The 'obvious' place to compromise frequently seems to win by some kind of default, as though there is simply no rationale for settling anywhere else."[26] The intrinsic rationale — especially the military rationale — for the Green Line may indeed be weak, but there is no other "obvious" place, and the Green Line, despite inevitable efforts by Israelis and Arabs to improve it, is therefore almost a predetermined outcome.

Marginal changes in the Green Line may be both desirable for Israel and achievable, especially if some reciprocity is admitted,[27] but at some point in the putative negotiations, Israel will almost surely have to make an agonizing strategic choice between the geomilitary value of the West Bank and Gaza and the political-security value of a peace settlement. At that point, the main considerations will be the extent to which the settlement implies a basic threat reduction to Israel and the extent to which residual threats can be dealt with by associated security measures. The political character of the settlement will bear directly on both considerations.

Nonterritorial settlements

The desire to reject this agonizing dilemma explains, in large measure, another type of golden mean — a solution that would bypass completely the question of territorial partition and provide, instead, for some kind of functional division of authority between Jews and Arabs (Palestinians and/or others). Nonterritorial settlements have the additional merit of avoiding the very difficult practical problems involved in the demarcation of separate jurisdictions for intermingled populations. Given the patchwork pattern of population distribution, no boundary line can be devised that will encompass the whole of any ethnonational group while simultaneously excluding all members of other groups.[28] Short of expulsion or genocide, ethnic heterogeneity will continue to be a fixture of the territory under discussion, and functional partition, on a communitarian basis, is therefore held by some to be the least disruptive means of accommodating the desires for collective self-expression of the different groups.[29]

Whatever the cogency of these considerations, the most appealing feature for Israelis of Palestinian self-rule in the West Bank and Gaza is its promise to relieve the burdens of occupation and to defuse the Palestinian issue without simultaneously ending Israeli control of the areas. Proposals for Palestinian self-rule within an Israeli context — sometimes referred to as "federal options" — can be conveniently grouped into four types:

(1) autonomy schemes, which would grant self-regulation to the Palestinians in the West Bank and Gaza in matters of personal status, education, religion, welfare, and certain types of economic activity and judicial affairs, but permit no separate status for these territories as political entities;
(2) federal schemes, which would establish a political entity (or entities) in the West Bank and Gaza separate from that of Israel, but reserve or assign authority to the institutions of the central (Israeli) government in the most critical functional areas;
(3) confederal schemes, which would provide an even greater de-

gree of autonomy for the constituent units by creating (or maintaining) their distinct international personalities, while permitting a division of power among them that may differ, in practice, only slightly from that of a federation; and,

(4) condominial schemes, which would formalize the de facto division of authority in the areas between Israel and Jordan, while conferring on West Bank and Gaza residents a greater degree of self-rule in local and regional affairs than is currently practiced.

On these main themes there are an almost infinite number of variations, with the different ideas being distinguished by the extent of devolution envisaged.[30] Their common point of departure, however, is that an Israeli or Israeli-dominated governing body retain ultimate control in the entire area west of the Jordan River. The exclusion of any other sovereignty from this area is often the implied purpose of Israeli proposals for self-rule; in some cases, as in the Likud government's approach to the autonomy question, it is the declared objective.[31] Since this latter position completely contradicts Arab expectations, it is not surprising that so little progress has been made in the negotiations with Egypt, or that no Palestinian interlocutor has yet shown any interest in joining these negotiations.

Federal options intended as alternatives to Israeli withdrawal, that is, as political settlements per se, are almost certain to be rejected by Palestinians, simply because their underlying assumption — that the political expression of national identity can be decoupled from territorial control — is anachronistic. This has been demonstrated, in the present context, at least since 1974 (that is, long before Sadat's visit to Jerusalem), when Israel actively began to explore the idea of "home rule" as a vehicle to avoid confronting the question of withdrawal, which would necessarily arise in any negotiations with either Jordan or the PLO. The initial Palestinian response in the territories was disinterest; it has subsequently developed into progressively more active resistance, and barring some unforeseeable reversal of contemporary norms of political identity, there is no reason to expect that such proposals will become more acceptable in the future.

Beyond the issue of attainability, however, there are serious grounds to question the fundamental soundness of nonterritorial settlements for this type of conflict. The character of the constituent elements makes the stability and durability of a settlement based on federal principles somewhat dubious. Even under the most propitious circumstances, when federalism attempts only to accommodate conflicting regional interests in large, but relatively homogeneous entities (for example, Federal Germany, Australia), the distribution of power and resources is a source of ongoing, if restrained, competition. When national, ethnic, linguistic, or religious conflicts are superimposed on these regional stresses, the problem of power-sharing is further exacerbated and itself frequently becomes a permanent focus of intrastate conflict.[32] In other words, federal regimes in ethnically divided societies replicate, in a "domestic" framework, the international conflict that preceded the institution of federalism, and simply create, in an age of national consciousness, another theater for war.

In this specific instance, a federal regime would not eliminate conflicts between Arabs and Jews; it would only internalize them. And the intensity of those conflicts would probably increase. Since no constitution could permanently satisfy the symbolic and material expectations of all parties, revisionist demands would inevitably arise. These might take the form either of a secessionist movement in the Arab-populated areas, or a generalized struggle for control over the central government. Such a struggle would be nourished by the increasing weight of the Arab population within the boundaries of the federal entity (particularly if the settlement also involved dealing with the Palestinian refugees by transferring some of them to areas of Arab self-rule), and perhaps by the re-engagement of other Arab states, as well. Even if the Palestinians failed to achieve their aims, the entity created by a federal solution would be condemned to perpetual strife. If the Palestinians were able to secede, the result, a product of bitter struggle, would be even less advantageous to Israel than a Palestinian state in the

West Bank and Gaza pursued through negotiations. And in the more unlikely eventuality that the Palestinians were able to take control of the entire apparatus, then it would be the Israelis, not the Palestinians, who would be left, at best, with some sort of limited communal self-rule. In either case, the institutional mechanisms of a federal solution, assuming it could be obtained, would prove to be an unreliable prophylactic against the dangers inherent in unilateral annexation of the West Bank and Gaza. Nonterritorial settlements do not, therefore, appear to offer either a preferable alternative to the status quo or a viable escape from the basic dilemma confronting Israel.

A non-PLO Israeli-Palestinian settlement

The strategic liabilities of nonsettlement and the problems associated with the search for a golden mean (territorial compromise or nonterritorial settlements) indicate that the implications of a settlement based on virtually complete Israeli withdrawal, despite its obvious drawbacks, must nevertheless be addressed. Such a settlement might be achieved in one of three ways.

The first could be a "Palestinian settlement" that excluded the PLO. This approach is grounded in the conviction that the raison d'être of that organization contradicts peaceful coexistence with Israel, and that PLO control of the West Bank and Gaza, under any circumstances, would constitute a source of postsettlement instability and danger. Israel should therefore prefer a settlement with reputedly more moderate Palestinians in the West Bank and Gaza, even if that settlement meant the creation of an independent Palestinian state in those areas.

The putative partners for Israel in this enterprise would be the so-called "third force" — a group of limited size and influence which stands between those in the territories loyal to the Hashemite regime of Jordan and those who support the PLO.[33] The third force bears a distinct Palestinian orientation; since the late 1960s, it has called for the creation of an independent "Palestinian entity" in the West Bank and Gaza and argued against the restoration of Jordanian rule. At the same time, it recognized early on the need to make peace with Israel, thereby acquiring a reputation for moderation or realism but also incurring the wrath of both Jordan and the PLO, as much for presuming to speak out independently and raising the specter of a "substitute leadership" (qiyada badila) as for substantive reasons. The third-force position was articulated after 1967 by such notables as the late Dr. Hamdi al-Taji al-Faruqi of al-Bira; 'Ayyub Musallam, a former mayor of Bethlehem; the Jerusalem journalist Muhammad Abu Shilbaya; and, with lesser consistency, the late Muhammad 'Ali al-Ja'bari, strongman of the Hebron region. Its most outspoken advocate has been the prominent Ramallah attorney 'Aziz Shahada.

Because of the overt moderation of the "third force," a settlement with this group might appear to be more easily attainable than one with the PLO. Moderate Palestinians in the West Bank and Gaza might be more prepared than the PLO to agree to terms advantageous to Israel, or even to be satisfied with some modified version of autonomy, at least on a temporary basis. Indeed, residents of the territories would probably be more concerned with their particularistic affairs than with the broader Palestinian question, and their localistic orientation and presumed sense of realism probably explain why Israel agreed at Camp David to include "Palestinians from the West Bank and Gaza Strip or other Palestinians as mutually agreed" in the Egyptian and proposed Jordanian delegations to the autonomy negotiations.

Optimism concerning the willingness or ability of third-force elements in the territories to conduct independent negotiations with Israel is probably unjustified. There were some tentative signs of local assertiveness immediately after President Sadat's visit to Jerusalem; these disappeared soon after Camp David, following vigorous counteraction by PLO supporters and a series of threats and assassinations against those who had expressed a readiness to investigate the possibilities of self-rule.[34] But even this brief flurry of independent expression constituted a deviation from the long-standing absence of vibrant indigenous political forces. For most of the post-1948 era, political power in the West Bank has tended to reflect relationships among Arab and other forces outside the area, rather than the distribution of opinions or resources within. Only the temporary chaos in the immediate aftermath of the 1967 War permitted the third force to emerge. Its visibility was greatest in the late 1960s; since then, local initiatives have become increasingly cautious and restrained — partly out of fear, partly out of genuine acceptance of the PLO as the sole legitimate representative of the Palestinians, partly out of frustration due to Israeli unresponsiveness to previous initiatives.[35] Some potential for independent action may yet remain. If the PLO, for example, rejected a settlement that promised to end the Israeli occupation, some local forces, armed with support from other Arab quarters, might summon up the will to discuss a separate agreement with Israel. But barring a radical change in the regional and international stature of the PLO, the prospect of significant local forces openly defying the PLO must be judged as quite remote. If local interlocutors become at all involved in negotiations with Israel, it would more likely be contingent on authorization and continuing direction by the PLO — in which case the non-PLO character of the settlement would become a legal fiction, perhaps temporarily useful in order to reduce domestic opposition but of no real long-term advantage to Israel.

However, the whole issue of the probability of a Palestinian settlement not involving the PLO is in some sense secondary. It is the comparative value of such a settlement, assuming that it is attainable, that should determine the advisability of pursuing this course. A settlement that bypassed the PLO would presumably be similar to a settlement negotiated with the PLO in terms of its territorial and other provisions and risk-minimization requirements. This is not just an assumption for purposes of analytical control; it reflects the high probability that Israel would have no reason to settle for less and that the Palestinian interlocutors would not or could not concede more. Any difference in the strategic value to Israel of a Palestinian settlement without the PLO would therefore be a function of its durability, that is, of the likelihood that its provisions would be upheld, and of the longer-term stability of the Palestinian state.

The potential benefit to Israel of a settlement contracted

directly with West Bank/Gaza negotiators derives from the particularistic perspective of the constituency they ostensibly represent. Either PLO or West Bank/Gaza negotiating partners
would be required to agree to complete peace and the renunciation of all further claims, but only for the constituents of the latter would Israeli withdrawal to the Green Line resolve direct
and immediate grievances in addition to the larger issue of national abnormality. There is therefore some reason to believe
that moderate West Bank/Gaza leaders would enter into a
peace agreement with fewer mental reservations. But the particularistic perspective of these leaders is, at the same time, a
liability for Israel because it limits their ability to legitimize a
final peace and undercuts their authority to settle the Palestinian
problem "in all its aspects."[36] The entire PLO, bypassed in the
settlement, would undoubtedly condemn it as capitulationist
and treasonous, and struggle to prevent its implementation.
Failing that, it might seek to undermine the government of the
new state and assume control itself.

PLO subversion of the peace or subsequent domination of
the Palestinian state is not foreordained. The provision for "participatory ratification" by the major Arab states raises the
possibility that the PLO, whose political and military power
depends in large measure on Arab indulgence or active support,
would be debilitated by the settlement, to the point where the
non-PLO leadership could enforce its rule. In the present circumstances, this possibility is not great. Most evidence still sup-
ports the contention that only "the representatives of the Palestinians [that is, the PLO] have it in their power to transmit the
relevant signal to pan-Arab sentiment."[37] That an attractive Israeli offer to non-PLO Palestinians might change this configuration cannot be excluded.

However, the marginal benefit to Israel of fewer mental reservations on the part of non-PLO rulers must be weighed
against the possibility that those rulers might yet be supplanted,
despite the change in the inter-Arab environment. In postindependence political struggles within the Palestinian state, an
unreconstructed PLO would be very well placed to raise the
"stab-in-the-back" theme in order to exploit inevitable social

strains and tensions, and this would probably strike a responsive chord among less privileged social strata and refugees already in the West Bank and Gaza, particularly among those subsequently resettled from other Arab countries. It is true that the same threat might conceivably be mounted by rejectionist splinters of the PLO itself against a PLO-endorsed peace, but the quantitative difference between this threat and that posed by a united PLO would be so great as to constitute a qualitatively different situation.

Thus, the main drawback of a settlement bypassing the PLO is that it would relieve the PLO mainstream of the necessity to purge itself of its absolutist ideology, its maximalist goals (especially refugee claims), and its extremist factions, and to confer its imprimatur on a settlement that inevitably requires wide-ranging Palestinian concessions. Within the foreseeable future, this drawback would appear to outweigh by far the potential benefit to Israel of attempting to exclude the PLO. In terms of its probable durability and political-strategic value to Israel, a Palestinian settlement without the PLO is therefore less desirable than one that directly implicates the PLO and diminishes its interest in, or capacity for, revisionism.

A non-Palestinian Israeli-Arab settlement

A second territorial approach for Israel might be to seek a direct settlement with other Arab actors in order to prevent the emergence of any Palestinian political entity. The underlying rationale of this approach would be the assumption that the history of the Israeli-Palestinian conflict is one of fundamental irreconcilability, that the two national movements are mutually exclusive, and that Palestinian (PLO or otherwise) rejection of Israel, notwithstanding any temporary political accommodation, is so deep-seated — almost primordial — that eventual resumption of the Palestinian assault against Israel's very existence is predetermined, subject only to ephemeral constraints of opportunity and circumstance. The hostility of non-Palestinian

Arabs, however, would presumably be dissipated more easily because it evolved at one remove from the initial conflict and is not rooted in direct material claims (land, property) against Israel within its pre-1967 frontiers.

This rationale explains, at least in part, the Israeli insistence after 1967 that only Jordan was a valid partner for discussions on the future disposition of the West Bank. And Jordan still remains the most visible and preferred alternative either to the so-called "Palestinian option"—in its PLO and other variants—or even, at least for the Labor party, to the continuation of the status quo.

If an Israeli-Arab settlement not only bypassed the Palestinians but also promised to eliminate their capacity to subvert it by suppressing their political and military institutions, it might merit serious consideration. Arab willingness and ability to ignore the Palestinian-national aspect of the conflict might counteract the consciousness and political assertiveness of the Palestinians to the point where they were assimilated into other societies or, at most, reduced to a cultural-folkloric entity (like the Circassians), with little prospect of realizing any political aspirations or seriously inconveniencing anyone else.

Needless to say, any Israeli-Arab settlement that failed to promise such an outcome, and especially any settlement in which the intended Arab outcome was precisely the opposite, would be extremely counterproductive for Israel. In such a settlement, Arab governments would essentially act as forwarding agents, securing the West Bank and Gaza from Israel and subsequently transmitting them to the Palestinians. The ostensible incentive for Israel would be political face-saving. It could withdraw from the territories without explicitly retreating from its refusal to agree to the creation of a Palestinian state.[38] Nevertheless, the ultimate outcome, despite the rationale for a settlement bypassing the Palestinians, would almost certainly be a Palestinian state, but with Israel deprived of both the geomilitary value of the territories and the political value of concessions—peace, recognition, risk-minimization provisions —extracted directly from the Palestinians. This outcome could be reversed through war, but it would surely be preferable to prevent it in advance by rejecting any Israeli-Arab settlement intended to secure a state for the Palestinians while allowing them to avoid the burden of peacemaking, and particularly one from which the PLO would benefit without being forced to negotiate with Israel. Such a settlement, when proposed by Arab advocates like Ihsan 'Abd al-Quddus,[39] merely constitutes an indirect approach to a Palestinian state, and its fundamental character would not change simply because of Israeli authorship.

In a non-Arab variation on the indirect settlement theme, the same drawback arises in an even more extreme form. According to one such variation, Israel would surrender the territories to a United Nations trustee, for a period ranging from six months to five years, during which time the Palestinians would organize and carry out political activity, culminating in a plebiscite on the future of the West Bank and Gaza. The purpose of this exercise, according to one unattributed report in a Saudi newspaper, would be to allow the Palestinians to receive control of the state directly from the United Nations, thus relieving the PLO of the problem of negotiating with and recognizing Israel.[40] The advantages to the PLO of such an arrangement are clear; they explain the efforts of Khalid al-Hasan, director of the Foreign Relations Department of the Palestine National Council, to mobilize European support in the spring of 1980 for a UN trusteeship.[41] But Israel would fail to secure, not only PLO concessions, but even direct negotiations with other Arab states. At best, Israel might obtain some UN commitments and guarantees. The distinction between this and unilateral withdrawal is meaningless.

Of all the alternative settlements not involving the Palestinians, the only one that appears to merit serious attention is therefore the "Jordanian option," that is, the restoration of the West Bank (perhaps together with the Gaza Strip) to Hashemite rule. Since the 1974 Rabat Summit Conference, and especially since the Baghdad Summit Conference in 1978, Jordanian leaders, including King Husayn himself, have repeatedly insisted that there is no longer a Jordanian option. Jordanian media, moreover, have explicitly endorsed the creation of a sovereign Palestinian state in the West Bank and Gaza. [42] At the same time, Jordanian involvement in the day-to-day affairs of the West Bank remains high. Jordan's attachment to the area, especially to Jerusalem, is constantly emphasized (pictures of the Dome of the Rock, for example, are screened throughout the day on Jordanian television). For these reasons, the possibility of a settlement based on the Jordanian option cannot be categorically excluded. Furthermore, many Israelis, especially in the Labor party, are convinced that *only* an agreement with Jordan could allow Israel to withdraw from the West Bank with a reasonable degree of security.

Any Israeli preference for a Jordanian over a Palestinian solution rests on a number of considerations beyond the basic belief that an Israeli-Palestinian rapprochement would be inherently transitory. These include the underlying logic of a reunification of the West and East Banks, in view of the intimate family and business ties that have been forged between them, as well as Husayn's attractiveness as a reputedly moderate, prowestern negotiating partner. A Jordanian regime in the West Bank and Gaza, moreover, might be a less powerful magnet for the political identity and loyalties of the Israeli Arabs. However, the most important factor is undoubtedly the vested Hashemite interest in regional stability. Despite its official policy, Jordan has reason to fear the potentially destabilizing impact of a Palestinian state on general grounds. Furthermore, the large Palestinian population in Transjordan and the possibility that a Palestinian state might view the East Bank, in addition to Israel, as Palestinian irredenta, suggest that Husayn might well be impelled to suppress any political expression of Palestinian consciousness. Because of his own Arab identity and the nature of his regime, he could probably do so more effectively than could Israel.

An agreement with Jordan could potentially satisfy the Israeli requirement that a settlement which excluded the Palestinians also eliminate their capacity to subvert it. Since this potential would not be very great unless that agreement were ratified by the other major Arab actors, Israel, like Jordan, would surely prefer broader Arab endorsement. Indeed, a Jordanian solution would probably resemble a Palestine-state solution in all major respects, including territorial, so that the major variable in determining its advisability for Israel remains, again, its likely sustainability. The Jordanian option must therefore be judged on the basis of its promise to generate a situation in which the overall character of Israeli-Arab relations, and the influence of Palestinians on those relations, are less threatening to Israel than are the implications of an independent Palestinian state.

One element in this calculation must be the likelihood that various risk-minimization provisions will be upheld. A Jordanian regime, for example, might find it easier to comply in the long run with arms limitations affecting only part of its state (the West Bank and Gaza) than would a Palestinian regime, whose entire state would be subject to those limitations. On the other hand, any subsequent Jordanian action (perhaps in response to domestic unrest) to reassert its sovereign rights and station additional forces or weapons on the West Bank would be politically difficult for Israel to oppose, given the formal state of peace. In view of Jordan's recognized sovereign status in the territories, an Israeli response to Jordanian violations of arms limitation provisions, particularly if they were "minor" and posed no qualitatively new danger to Israeli security, would be technically permissible but politically problematic. Diplomatic considerations (for example, appeals to avoid further escalation of tensions) would suggest restraint, and domestic considerations might also preclude military action containing risks "disproportionate" to the provocation, with immobilism being the likely outcome.[43] It is true that a Palestinian state might also be tempted to exceed permissible force levels, but concern about its own independence might well dissuade it from inviting foreign Arab troops into its territory — and these, at least for the foreseeable future, would constitute a much greater threat to Israel than any indigenous Palestinian military buildup.

However, the most critical variable of a Jordanian solution would be its underlying stability and durability, that is, its effect on Palestinian political motivations and capabilities. An examination of this variable must be related to the specific character of Jordanian rule and inter-Arab politics in the postsettlement environment. One possibility is that the regime would revive the integrationist approach toward the Palestinians that prevailed before 1967. In this case, the West Bank would have no separate administrative existence, the political status of Jerusalem would be downgraded, and every effort would be made to suppress expressions of Palestinian identity and erase a particularistic Palestinian conciousness. The post-1967 process of Palestinization would be reversed, the national dimension of the "Palestine problem" might fade into obscurity, and the Palestinians themselves would, if this approach succeeded, eventually assimilate into the Jordanian entity. Given the linguistic and religious-cultural proximity of Palestinians and Jordanians, and the end of the Israeli occupation that did so much to stimulate Palestinian identity, such an outcome would not be altogether inconceivable, especially if other Arab states adopted a similar integrationist approach toward their own Palestinian populations. However, the vicissitudes of inter-Arab politics and the temptation to exploit an unresolved Palestine problem would probably make an all-Arab commitment to do so unreliable and, as dangerous from Israel's perspective, unenforceable. Furthermore, the subjective factors of Palestinian identity (historical experience, political consciousness, and so on) could not be quickly extinguished, and might in fact be further inflamed by a peace settlement viewed as unequivocally anti-Palestinian.

Thus, Husayn recognized even in 1972 that it would be futile to attempt simply to restore the political status quo ante bellum in a reunified Jordan. Nothing since then has made a distinctive Palestinian consciousness more delible, and Jordanian rule would therefore more probably conform to the logic of federation that Husayn espoused in 1972 — that is, it would accept the inevitability of a Palestinian identity and attempt to accommodate it through some structural arrangement short of complete independence. The 1972 proposal called for a United Arab Kingdom consisting of a Palestinian region in the West Bank (and "other liberated Palestinian territories") and a Jordanian region in the East Bank. Jerusalem would serve as the Palestinian regional capital; Amman would be the capital of the Jordanian region and the central capital of the kingdom. Each region would have its own executive, legislative, and judicial authorities, staffed by residents of that region, but there would also be a central executive authority (responsible for "the kingdom's security, stability, and prosperity"), a central legislature (with equal regional representation), and a central supreme court. The king would be head of state and supreme commander of the unified armed forces.[44]

Husayn's scheme for a United Arab Kingdom, or any other proposal for Palestinian self-rule in Jordan, would confront, albeit in a less extreme form, the same challenge facing Israeli federal options — locating the precise balance between devolution sufficient to satisfy Palestinian demands for self-expression and central control sufficient to prevent secession or a Palestinian overthrow of the regime. Without the former, internal stability in Jordan, hence, the stability of Israeli-Arab relations, would be threatened; without the latter, any presumed advantage for Israel in dealing with Husayn, rather than directly with the PLO, would be illusory. Needless to say, the correct formula would be extremely elusive and delicate; Israeli reliance on its being identified and maintained would be an unusual act of faith.

For as long as Palestinians and Transjordanians (especially bedouin and southern East Bank elites) retained different collective self-identities and collective visions of Jordan's proper image, the federal structure would only disguise an ongoing competition for dominance, expressed in a struggle over the institutions of the central government — key cabinet posts, the army command, the security services, and the Royal Court. Given the large Palestinian presence in the East Bank, this struggle may be inevitable regardless of the disposition of the West Bank and Gaza. If those areas became an independent state, the instruments of state control in the hands of Palestinian leaders might well improve their capacity to agitate Palestinians in the East Bank and undermine Hashemite control there; the incorporation of the territories — with their 1.2 million Palestinian inhabitants — into the Jordanian body politic would surely strengthen the Palestinian side in any domestic struggle. And the liquidation of the refugee problem (without which the question of Palestine could not be resolved) would only further increase the danger to the Jordanian regime of demographic Pal-estinization, perhaps at a rate exceeding that of Palestinian acquiescence in the political settlement. (In view of this dilemma, Jordan may well prefer the status quo to any settlement at all.)

It is possible, despite these inauspicious circumstances, that the Hashemite regime would continue to prevail and would be able to maintain the peace, especially if its agreement with Israel received prior pan-Arab legitimation. If it decided to pursue the Jordanian option, Israel would therefore probably require the repeal of the 1974 Rabat Summit decision designating the PLO as the "sole legitimate spokesman" of the Palestinians, together with an explicit Arab authorization for Jordan to negotiate peace. But it is also possible that internal instability and conflict would intensify to the point where Palestinian opposition became containable at a cost no longer reasonable in Hashemite eyes. In that case, the final result of the Jordanian option would be a Palestinian state, either on the West Bank (through secession or voluntary devolution) or on both Banks (through takeover). The risks to the Hashemite regime, in either case, are sufficiently daunting to suggest that Jordanian repudiation of the Jordanian option is rather more sincere than many Israelis are inclined to believe.

The danger to Israel itself, however, is just as clear and even more germane to the present analysis, namely, that the transmission of the West Bank (with or without Gaza) to Jordan will ultimately produce an independent Palestinian state that is bound by no commitments to or recognition of Israel and subject to no internal or external constraints other than the military balance. All this would take place in an Arab-Israeli environment in which the Palestine issue had been revived, perhaps in a more virulent form than ever. If this state were confined to the West Bank, the result for Israel would be at least as menacing as would a radical takeover of a Palestinian state originally conceived in peace; if the Jordanian option resulted in a hostile Palestinian state on both Banks, the threat would grow accordingly.

4

Security Implications of an
Independent Palestinian State

The third territorial alternative for Israel would be a peace settlement contracted directly with the PLO that provided for an
independent Palestinian state in the West Bank and Gaza. Some
of the risks and opportunities associated with a Palestine-state
settlement derive specifically from involvement of the PLO;
others are implied in the creation of a Palestinian state under
any circumstances. But even these risks and opportunities are
liable to be most sharply pronounced in the case of an Israeli-
PLO agreement, and the entire range of considerations is
therefore addressed in this context.

All of the potential security risks to Israel of a Palestine-state
settlement can be subsumed under the single rubric of "instability." A peace settlement which, because of the character or
policies of a Palestinian state, was inherently unstable, would be
a permanent source of insecurity. Constant tensions would prevent the normalization of Israeli-Palestinian and Israeli-Arab
relations. Instead, the regional landscape would be marred by
security incidents — contrived or spontaneous. In an atmosphere
of twilight peace, incidents might easily escalate, by accident or
by design, into large-scale hostilities, with Israel deprived of
both the geomilitary benefits of the West Bank and many of the
anticipated political-strategic benefits of withdrawal.

Consensus in Israel about the instability of peace postulated
on a Palestinian state is based on a number of elements:

(1) the ideological and practical obstacles to Palestinian recon-
    ciliation with Israel and the consequent danger that the

mental reservations of Palestinian leaders would inevitably produce an irredentist state consciously committed to the continuation of the struggle for maximal Palestinian objectives — in short, the risk of a "purposeful" confrontation state;

(2) the political, economic, and social obstacles to domestic stability in a Palestinian state and the consequent danger, regardless of any inclination in favor of coexistence, that an outlet for systemic disorders would eventually be sought in a renewal of the conflict with Israel — in short, the risk of an "accidental" confrontation state;

(3) the persistence of inter-Arab rivalries and Soviet designs on the region and the consequent danger that other Arab states and/or the Soviet Union, still hopeful of exploiting residual hostility toward Israel, would provoke a nonaggressive Palestinian government into greater belligerency or else subvert it in favor of more radical and pliable forces — in short, the risk of an "enlisted" confrontation state.[1]

Any or all of these factors could undermine the peace and produce a variety of security threats, ranging from terrorist attacks (supported by the Palestinian state or in defiance of it) to a full-scale coordinated Arab assault on Israel, using the West Bank as a springboard.

Furthermore, a Palestinian state might be able to expand eastward and take over Jordan. This could intensify the security risks to Israel by increasing the human and material resources at the Palestinians' disposal. On the other hand, the union of the two Banks might expose the Palestinian-dominated state to domestic disruption (as a result of unrest among East Bank Jordanians), thus weakening that state's cohesion and capacity to act against Israel. At worst, a Palestinian takeover of Jordan might therefore add to Palestinian capabilities, but it would not introduce a qualitatively different kind of security threat.

In addition to the security dimension, a Palestinian state implies some potentially adverse consequences for other Israeli interests. Palestinian statehood in the West Bank and Gaza might act as a magnet for nationalist sentiments among Israeli Arabs and a stimulant, passive or active, of secessionist tendencies in areas like the Western Galilee, where the Arab population is concentrated. It would almost certainly alter the current status of Jerusalem and of Israeli settlements in the territories, either as a condition or consequence of peace. And in the economic sphere, Palestinian statehood might restrict access to an important Israeli market, deprive Israel of a source of manpower, and threaten some of Israel's water supplies.

All of these risks are possible. The mere reiteration of conceivable danger, however, is both superficial and politically sterile. A functional evaluation of the consequences of a Palestinian state must attempt to assess the probability that these dangers would materialize, the conditions that would contribute to threat-minimization, and the countermeasures currently or prospectively available to Israel.

Palestine as a purposeful confrontation state

Doubts about the ultimate willingness of a Palestinian state to co-exist peacefully with Israel are grounded in the history of the Palestinian national movement. For over sixty years, since the beginning of Jewish-Arab confrontation in Palestine, the dominant tendency in Palestinian politics has always been one of rejectionism. Palestinian reconciliation with the Jewish state would therefore constitute a reversal of historic proportions, and it is precisely because of the magnitude of this reversal that the credibility of any Palestinian agreement to peace is often viewed with such skepticism. This skepticism is reinforced by the professions of many PLO leaders that a state would not constitute a final solution of the Palestinian problem, but merely a stage in the Palestinian struggle, a tactical measure to facilitate the ultimate objective—the total liberation of Palestine. The "strategy of stages" is, indeed, the very core of PLO policy, and it has been upheld with such consistency and tenacity that any hypothetical verbal retreat on this point would be highly suspect.[2]

There are serious grounds for concern about the reliability of Palestinian commitments and the sincerity of Palestinian intentions. These do not derive simply from the general theoretical problem of perpetual peace; that relations have, in other situations, deteriorated after decades or even centuries of relative stability is irrelevant to the time frame in which decisionmakers must operate. Nor is the issue one of some purported sociocultural predisposition among Arabs either to honor or to violate international agreements; in this regard, the historical record of Arab states has been mixed, that is, not significantly different from that of other international actors. Instead, the problem is a specific function of the extent to which Palestinian renunciations of claims against Israel within the Green Line would be devalued, for ideological or practical reasons, by mental reservations.

There have been some rather ambiguous pronouncements on this issue. Some PLO leaders have argued that a Palestinian state would continue the struggle against Israel, but that political means (diplomacy, propaganda, and so forth), rather than armed struggle, would be emphasized after a settlement.[3] Such behavior would still constitute a danger to Israel, because of its potential to escalate, but it would be a less threatening proposition than the perpetuation of violent confrontation. There have also been far less equivocal statements by prominent Palestinian leaders within the occupied territories. Even those who openly declare their allegiance to the PLO and are considered radical by the Israeli authorities have occasionally expressed willingness to coexist in peace with Israel.[4] Nevertheless, statements by PLO officials of an unqualified readiness to coexist in peace with Israel are so rare that they border on eccentricity.[5]

Differences in substance or even in nuance reflect a degree of programmatic uncertainty quite remote from the ideological rigidity of "official" documents and pronouncements. They also indicate an existential contradiction between major segments of the Palestinian people. The establishment of an independent state would satisfy the collective political grievance of the Palestinians — national abnormality — but by ending the Israeli occupation of the West Bank and Gaza, it would relieve the practical dilemma only of those Palestinians living in those territories. For the rest, the existence of Israel would continue to constitute a frustration of their desire to return — to the place and condition of their lives before 1948. With the passage of time, the refugees of 1948, especially those who remained in the camps, naturally tended to embellish and idealize their vision of life before 1948. Among these refugees, especially among those old enough to have a conscious memory of that life (the "generation of Palestine"), the cause of Palestine is as much a struggle for the restoration of "Paradise Lost," an attachment to a specific home or plot of earth, as it is a struggle for the normalization of the Palestinians' national status.[6]

An independent state in the West Bank and Gaza could not satisfy the "village patriotism" of these people, because it would be a political response irrelevant to their concrete aspirations. These village patriots are the major constituency for Palestinian maximalism today and they would remain an obstacle to the routinization of Israeli-Palestinian peace after a settlement. Some of them might actually direct the affairs of the Palestinian state, since many PLO leaders come from inside the Green Line and themselves embody this very personal perspective on the insufficiency of a Palestine-state solution.[7]

The problem is best illustrated by Palestinian insistence that the "right to return" is inalienable. Even in statements intended to emphasize the progressive moderation of Palestinian positions, the right to return is consistently recalled as a just demand, regardless of political arrangements between Israel and a Palestinian state.[8] The return of the Palestinians to their pre-1948 idyl is impossible — physically, because many of the villages they inhabited no longer exist and the towns are changed beyond all recognition; politically, because their introduction into Israel would derange the basic character of Israeli society and thus negate one of the primary purposes of Israeli withdrawal from the West Bank and Gaza. Nevertheless, it is unrealistic to expect that any formal peace document will completely dissolve Palestinian reservations and lead to the abandonment of all hopes for "total liberation." At best, the attitude may emerge that prevailed in France after 1871 vis-à-vis Alsace-Lorraine: *Parlez-y jamais, pensez-y toujours.*

However, the operational question for Israeli policymakers should not be abstract Palestinian preferences, but rather whether those preferences are likely to be programmatic as well as ideological. If a Palestinian state were subject to so many systemic constraints — internal and regional — that confrontation was seen as futile or counterproductive, the ideology of liberation and return might, over time, fade into ritual incantation and be of no substantive importance. Thus, the central calculation for Israel should be whether a Palestinian state would be more likely, in practice, to serve as a stimulus to or a substitute for the maximal objective, whether it would produce a regional matrix that would facilitate or impair the active pursuit of irredentist aims.

Uncertainty over the practical consequences of a West Bank/ Gaza Strip state has bedeviled the attitudes of Palestinians themselves. Those who believe that an independent state would facilitate additional claims on Israel base their optimism on a number of factors, including the advantages to be derived from a secure base and control of state resources. Statehood might change the role of the Palestinians in inter-Arab rivalries, from that of an exploited object to that of a full-fledged participant, with enhanced capacity to elicit active Arab support for subsequent Palestinian demands. A particularly weighty consideration in Palestinian eyes may be the expected impact on Israel of a reversal of the historical course of Israeli-Palestinian relations. Israeli withdrawal from the territories would constitute a retreat of major proportions that might arrest the dynamic of Zionist success. According to a widespread Arab perception, Israel is an inherently artificial entity, full of internal contradictions which can be contained only by the war against the Arabs. Once this bond is removed, by a political settlement that reverses the momentum of Zionism, Israel will be ripe for spontaneous disintegration, catalyzed, if necessary, by a resumption of the Palestinian struggle through political, moral, and psychological means. In short, a Palestinian state may promise the eventual withering away of Israel.[9]

On the other hand, both the detractors and the supporters of the ministate recognize that raison d'état might very well militate against further struggle and effectively preclude the possibility of realizing ultimate goals. More specifically, it has been argued that an independent state would debilitate the Palestinian national movement internally, create a more identifiable and accessible, hence, vulnerable base, divert Palestinian efforts and resources, diminish Arab and international support for the Palestinian cause, and introduce an enfeebling element of caution into Palestinian politics because of fear of jeopardizing the little that would have been achieved.[10] Some of these anticipated consequences flow from the symbolism of a peace agreement and Palestinian recognition of Israel, which is precisely why these conditions are rejected even by PLO "moderates"; others ensue from the probable dynamics of government decisionmaking, that is, the burden of responsible cost-benefit calculation that state- and regime-maintenance entail.

Perhaps the most profound impact would be on the continued vigor of the Palestinian movement itself. A major source of the PLO's strength is its ability to present a facade of Palestinian unity, despite the potentially contradictory interests of various Palestinian constituencies, on the basis of a set of demands which are all, at present, hypothetical. So long as complete liberation, the right of return, creating a state, and ending the Israeli occupation are all out of reach, there is no need to choose between them, no compulsion to sacrifice some objectives in order to attain or preserve others, and no impediment to mutual support by the different constituencies immediately associated with these demands. But an independent state would change this configuration. Those whose direct needs had been satisfied first — the West Bank and Gaza Palestinians eager to end the occupation — would be reluctant to endanger that achievement and inclined to resist others intent on pursuing the struggle.[11] Those whose demands for a normalization of the Palestinians' international status induce them to accept "the compromise on behalf of a ministate, a passport, a flag, a nationality"[12] would hesitate to risk that status by endorsing an adventurous initiative against Israel. This category would undoubtedly include a substantial number of Palestinians — refugees who have already established reasonably satisfactory personal lives elsewhere as well as those who may be resettled inside or outside the West Bank/Gaza as part of the peace agreement.

After the establishment of an independent state, these constituencies would have a vested interest in checking any potential adventurism on the part of Palestinian maximalists, who would presumably consist of "village patriots" and "ideological rejectionists." It is, of course, impossible to predict with certainty the outcome of a struggle between the two camps. Nevertheless, there is reason to believe that the "accommodationists" would prevail over the maximalists, primarily because of structural weaknesses in the latter camp.

Insofar as the village patriots are concerned, the decoupling of their individual claims from the national dimension of the Palestine issue would probably diminish pan-Arab and Palestinian support for their claims; and material compensation may reduce the intensity with which they themselves espouse the return. Most important, the generation of Palestine has, with the passage of time, become a progressively smaller element within the Palestinian population.

Although no reliable figures for global Palestinian population exist, a reasonable estimate would be approximately 3.5 million.[13] Of these, refugees who might have personal memories of the areas that became Israel in 1948, that is, those now over the age of thirty-five, constitute only about 10-11 percent; camp residents of this age group make up less than 4 percent of the total.[14] For purely actuarial reasons, this generation, the human hard-core of the impulse to return, will continue to dwindle and will eventually disappear.

The role and presumptive strength of the rejectionists is somewhat more ambiguous. To the extent that rejectionism implies a principled unwillingness to accommodate Israel as a permanent reality, despite any transitory political arrangements, all the major Palestinian institutions are rejectionist. In this sense, the problem of rejectionism is simply a variation on the "mental reservations" theme, which has already been discussed. However, rejectionism has a more limited meaning — the refusal to make the practical concessions necessary to secure Israeli withdrawal in favor of a Palestinian state. Even in this sense, the

PLO and all its member organizations are officially rejectionist, and only a retreat from this position would make a Palestinian state possible. If such a retreat comes about at all, it will probably be undertaken by the *Fatah* "mainstream" of the PLO, supported by independents (including representatives from the territories), Communists, and perhaps by *Sa'iqa*, if the settlement is endorsed by Syria. Those to whom the appellation "rejectionist" is restricted, erroneously, in current usage — the Popular Front for the Liberation of Palestine (PFLP), the Iraqi-sponsored Arab Liberation Front, and other factions — could then be expected immediately to resist the "capitulation" by violent means. If they prevailed, the settlement would not be implemented and Israel would have lost nothing, except perhaps a measure of international opprobrium engendered by its present posture; if they were crushed, their residual capacity to destabilize future relations could be contained fairly well by Palestinian authorities enjoying the resources of a state apparatus and the support of significant elements in the Palestinian public. Indeed, the most ominous danger sign would not be a violent split in Palestinian ranks before the settlement were implemented, but rather abstention by the rejectionists, which would indicate an intention to keep their forces intact with the hope of infiltrating and taking over the state at some future stage. It is not likely, however, that such a prospect would escape the attention of the "capitulationists."

Thus, the creation of a Palestinian state conditioned on mutual recognition and peaceful coexistence with Israel would quite probably split the Palestinian population, enfeeble the PLO, reduce the intensity of collective commitment to maximal goals, and debilitate the national movement by coopting, isolating, or eliminating the most logical sources of future revisionism.

Palestinian willingness to pursue a strategy of stages would be further inhibited by the vulnerability of their base of operations. A state might enhance conventional Palestinian military capabilities, but it would also constitute a discrete and accessible target for Israel; it might perhaps be expanded by aggressive behavior, but given the balance of forces between Israel and a

West Bank/Gaza state, at least for the foreseeable future, it would more likely be diminished, or even eliminated, as a result of armed conflict.

Any hopes for more favorable Palestinian prospects would necessarily rest on a measure of active external support and involvement. But foreign sympathy for the Palestinian cause, at least in those countries where perceptions of equity or justice play some role in influencing policy, is likely to diminish once that cause has been transformed, by the creation of a Palestinian state, from the struggle of a homeless people for self-determination into an expansionist, irredentist crusade. The position of the Soviet Union and its clients, of course, would not be affected by such considerations, and the possibility of Soviet support for Palestinian revisionism is self-evident. However, Soviet involvement, though a serious danger for Israel, would be primarily a function of superpower relations in the region, regardless of whether it were prompted by Palestinian appeals or by Soviet initiatives. Its probability will be assessed in the latter context.

The most problematic and critical variable would be the material contribution of other Arab states to a Palestinian-inspired confrontation with Israel. Palestinians might be reluctant to solicit such support, since it could compromise their sovereignty or produce a military conflict in which Palestinian independence would be the first casualty, whatever the final outcome. And even if practical Arab support for Palestinian revisionism were actively sought, it is not at all clear that this support would be forthcoming. Historically, the Arab effort on behalf of Palestine was wholly resolute only when the direct interests of Arab states were engaged.[15] Even today, the unwillingness of Arab states to expend their national resources, aside from rhetoric, and risk their immediate interests for the sake of Palestine is a source of bitter disappointment to the Palestinians themselves.[16]

The impact of a Palestinian state on Arab attitudes to Israel and on the centrality of the Palestine issue in inter-Arab politics cannot be known. It is reasonable to expect, however, that in the aftermath of a settlement, the Palestinian capacity to mobilize Arab assistance would be further weakened. The satisfaction, even if partial, of Palestinian national aspirations, would undercut the moral basis of their claim on Arab resources. The reduction of the Palestinian presence in various Arab states — through voluntary and/or compulsory evacuation or through rehabilitation of refugees — would diminish their ability to coerce support from fragile governments, especially in Lebanon and the Gulf. The "normalization" of the Palestinians' condition would transform them into a "normal" actor in the interplay of Arab politics, that is, one whose capacity to influence the behavior of other actors rests primarily on its instrumental resources (military power, economic assets, geographic advantage, and so on) rather than on ideological privilege or preeminence. Relations of influence based on these factors suggest that a Palestinian state bent on confrontation with Israel would find it difficult to impose its demands on other states with whom prior coordination was sought; a unilateral provocation, based on the hope that other states would be compelled by Arab solidarity to intervene, would be extremely hazardous.

Those Arab states with the greatest potential influence on a Palestinian state — Jordan, Egypt, and, for financial reasons, Saudi Arabia — are precisely those with the most to fear from regional conflict and Palestinian-inspired instability, and they could be expected to disengage from the conflict, and even to restrain Palestinian "irresponsibility," once a PLO-endorsed settlement provided them with the requisite moral fig leaf.[17] Jordan, in particular, would be very concerned about the direction of a Palestinian state's policy, since its own survival as a separate entity could be threatened by a reactivation of the Palestine issue, and it would have every reason to use its own considerable levers of influence (Palestinian assets in the East Bank and, especially, control of physical access from the West Bank to the eastern Arab world) in order to temper the behavior of the Palestinian state. More distant Arab states, like Libya or Iraq, might display greater responsiveness to Palestinian appeals, either out of ideological sympathy or to promote their claims of leadership in the Arab world, despite the diminished political utility of such a posture in a postsettlement environment. Still, the very distance that reduces the vulnerability of these states to the risks of renewed Arab-Israeli conflict also limits their ability to alter appreciably any Israeli-Palestinian balance of forces.

The role of Syria in this projected constellation of forces is most ambiguous. Syria is currently the leading force in the Arab "National Front of Steadfastness and Confrontation," and its hostility to a political settlement is so intense that it has challenged its main financial benefactor, Saudi Arabia, over a Saudi political proposal containing a very noncommittal endorsement of the principle "that all states in the region should be able to live in peace."[18] It has also threatened war with Jordan out of fear that King Husayn was contemplating reviving the Jordanian option, and it has even, according to some reports, decided to terminate 'Arafat's leadership of the PLO because of his excessive "moderation."[19] Its proximity, its military power, its ability to provide access for other Arab forces, and its influence over events in Lebanon give Syria a significant capacity either to block a peace settlement or to undermine it ex post facto — alone or in combination with a revisionist Palestinian state. And without a simultaneous settlement of the Israeli-Syrian conflict, Syria would have every incentive to act in just this manner. However, if the application of Israeli law to the Golan Heights were not to prove an insuperable obstacle to Israeli-Syrian accommodation, then the postsettlement Syrian calculus might more closely approximate that of Egypt, Jordan, and Saudi Arabia. Syrian willingness, for reasons of state, to move decisively against Palestinian challenges to Syrian interests was demonstrated in the Syrian invasion of Lebanon in 1976, and the possibility of future Syrian-Israeli cooperation, even if tacit, in containing potentially dangerous behavior by a Palestinian state cannot be excluded.[20] For these reasons, an explicit Syrian imprimatur of the Israeli-Palestinian settlement, though it also implies a change in the current status of the Golan Heights, would be highly desirable. Even without Syrian ratification of the peace, Egyptian, Jordanian, and Saudi adherence to the agreement would reduce the effectiveness of Syrian opposition and the danger of a Palestine-centered war coalition.

But a settlement that also minimized parochial Syrian incentives to support Palestinian irredentism would be clearly superior to one that did not.

In either case, a Palestinian state, for both internal and external reasons, is quite liable to be severely constrained in its ability to mount an effective struggle for maximal objectives, whatever the mental reservations of its leaders. A posture of confrontation, consciously pursued, is therefore not indicated by a rational calculation of the circumstances — costs and benefits, risks and opportunities — that Palestinian decisionmakers would probably face. There remains, however, an additional danger for Israel, namely, that Palestinian decisionmakers, despite every logical reason to the contrary, would nevertheless act irrationally and embark on a confrontationist course. Despite the widespread conviction that power and office necessarily produce responsible behavior, there are enough examples of irresponsible rulers, or even of "crazy states," to justify some skepticism. [21]

"Craziness" means behavior that is impossible to explain or predict using the logic of conventional strategic analysis. It can be characterized on a number of dimensions (goal content, goal commitment, risk propensity, means-goals relationship, style) and it may result in actions extremely destructive to targets of the crazy actor's wrath, as well as to the actor himself. The probability of its incidence is, by definition, difficult to measure, but a number of clues may nevertheless exist. Of the factors that are said to increase the possibility of craziness (disillusionment with contemporary values, frustration of minimal aspirations, feelings of externally caused deprivation, availability of mass mind-control or suggestion devices), at least two, and perhaps three, are political-cultural, and are more likely to be found in nonstate organizations or millenarian movements than in national governments. [22] Indeed, it may not be coincidental that most of the historical examples of craziness cited in the crazy-state model are actually of nonstate actors — Crusades, Muslim Holy Wars, the Mahdi revolt in the Sudan, the Assassins, transnational terror groups, and so on. Only Nazi Germany and, with some qualification, pre-World War II Japan are recalled as concrete manifestations of crazy states. Furthermore, when crazy individuals or movements have taken over a state apparatus, they have usually abandoned their craziness (for example, the Mau Mau in Kenya) or concentrated on internal terror, which may be irrational and morally intolerable (for example, Idi Amin, Jean Bokassa, Khmère Rouge) but constitutes no mortal danger to immediate neighbors or to the international system.

Finally, the impact of crazy actors depends on their physical capacity to do damage to other states. A Palestinian state, even if free of all contractual limitations, would be a microstate in terms of self-generated military capacity. Its damage potential would be primarily subconventional (sporadic terrorism) or superconventional (biological, chemical, nuclear), probably in a catalytic role. But with the possible exception of the nuclear dimension, a Palestinian state would not necessarily be superior to a nonstate Palestinian national movement in its external action capabilities, whereas it would be more vulnerable and more unlikely, for reasons already discussed, to behave in crazy ways. In short, a crazy Palestinian state's "expected impact significance" (a joint function of probability and external impact)[23] must be judged lower than that of the PLO's in the absence of a settlement.

Although explicit Palestinian renunciation of maximal claims against Israel would not completely eliminate mental reservations, it would have a significant impact on Palestinian ideology. More important, while the possibility that a Palestinian state would be confrontationist cannot be categorically excluded, the conditions and consequences of its creation would impair its subsequent ability and willingness to pursue an actively revisionist policy.

Palestine as an accidental confrontation state

Even if the sincerity of a Palestinian commitment to peace were beyond question, the political capacity of a Palestinian state in the West Bank and Gaza to sustain this commitment is uncertain. Inevitable problems of institution-building, social integration, and economic development would pose a challenge to the stability of the Palestinian political system, raising the possibility that beleaguered Palestinian authorities might seek in adventurous foreign policies a diversion for domestic discontent.

This danger lies at the heart of assertions that a Palestinian state would not be viable. The notion of viability is much abused, and immaterial. No definitive specification of the irreducible physical or cultural attributes of statehood has been formulated, and states that might appear to lack even the minimal requisites of feasibility nevertheless manage to survive. The real issue is the extent to which domestic instability would be fueled by dissatisfaction over the distribution of political and material benefits, and how this instability would affect relations with Israel. Some instability is inevitable. The potential for it exists in every state, as it surely would in a Palestinian state. But only if it were to overflow the borders of that state—in the form of a belligerent foreign policy or, alternatively, of a political vacuum inviting intervention by outside powers—might it set off a dynamic of regional tensions which, through escalation, could pose a threat to the security of other regional actors, including Israel.

Despite widespread discussion of the possible impact of a Palestinian state, systematic attention has not been paid—with a few notable exceptions—to the probable nature of its political and economic regime, or to the question of domestic stability in general. With regard to the political dimension, the hope has been expressed, particularly inside the occupied territories, that the postindependence regime would be democratic and pluralistic. According to one source, West Bank and Gaza intellectuals foresee "a representative republic, perhaps presidential rather than parliamentary, based on popular participation in government with the right to vote guaranteed for both men and women. The political system of the Palestinian state would be more like Israel's than that existing in Arab societies."[24]

In view of the experience of other newly independent states in the Third World, and particularly in the Arab world, a democratic regime in Palestine would appear to be counterintuitive. Palestinians sometimes ground their optimism in the uniqueness of the Palestinian experience, and emphasize such

factors as the prevalence of higher education, the acquisition of
administrative skills in the service of other states, or even "the
effect of Palestinian suffering."[25] The relevance of these factors
to the entrenchment of democratic values is unclear, and a more
skeptical prognosis suggests that the state would be governed by
leaders of the PLO, who have been inevitably "imbued with
conspiratorial methods and clandestine behavior."[26] In fact, the
lack of a tradition of participatory democracy among the Palestinians themselves, as well as the patterns established in
analogous societies elsewhere, militate against the emergence of
liberal democracy in an independent Palestine. However, the
immediate issue here is not the particular form of the regime,
but rather its prospects for stability, and here the picture is
much more ambiguous.

A similar confusion applies to the economic dimension.
Many Palestinians, especially merchants and manufacturers,
desire a free-enterprise, capitalist economy, for both business
and nationalist reasons, that is, in order to attract foreign in-
vestors.[27] However, the magnitude of the developmental and
social welfare effort anticipated, particularly if large numbers of
refugees are to be rehabilitated, indicates that central planning
and state control will necessarily characterize the economy, at
least in the early years. Still, the important question in the present context is not the coloration of the economic regime, but
rather its relative capacity to satisfy the expectations of the Palestinian public, and on this issue, external variables will be of
critical importance. In short, assumptions about the political
and economic temper of a Palestinian state need to be explored
in greater detail.

Political challenges to Palestinian stability

A Palestinian state would embark on its independent career
with a number of significant advantages. Foremost among these
would be a relatively homogeneous population, at least in the
ethnolinguistic sense. The entire population would be Arabic-
speaking, and at least 95 percent would be Muslim, of the Sunni
variant.[28] Thus, a Palestinian state would at least not suffer the

confessional factionalism that has torn Lebanon apart and periodically erupted in Egypt; nor would it encounter the ethnic-confessional divisiveness that burdens the political systems of Iraq and Syria. In addition, a Palestinian state could draw on a cadre of educated and experienced civil servants, and would not have to depend on large numbers of foreign experts who might create a focus of nativist resentment, as they have sometimes done in other newly independent states, and as Palestinians themselves have done in some Arab countries.[29]

Nevertheless, some political obstacles to Palestinian stability are potentially serious. Underlying all of these is the absence of a prior history of political sovereignty, even in the remote past. Without traditional sources of legitimation for political structures and modes of behavior, a Palestinian political consensus on these issues would have to be created ab initio, and this process would inevitably be attended by uncertainties, discontinuities, and internal conflicts. After the euphoria of independence wore off, Palestinians would have to begin to grapple with the more mundane functions of normal political systems — interest articulation and aggregation, leadership selection, and conflict adjudication. Unless and until legitimate political institutions exist to perform these functions, demands might well exceed the capacity of the system to satisfy them, and the stability of the state would be tenuous.

There is little doubt that the system would be burdened by heavy demands for representation and participation. Palestinian political consciousness and mobilization are high — the result of widespread education, exposure to communications media, urbanization, and a tradition of geographical and social mobility, all of which have been accelerated by the refugee experience since 1948. Therefore, the debate on the fundamental issues of politics — who rules, by what means, for which purposes — would probably be intense, sharp, and perhaps bloody, before a sustainable formula to deal with these questions emerged.

Conflict could be expected simultaneously along a number of axes: ideological, personal, class, and regional. The sources of ideological conflict are perhaps most salient, since they relate to the essential character of the state. The question of the state's conscious posture toward Israel has been assumed, for purposes of analysis, to have been resolved—one way or another—in favor of nonconfrontation. A number of other potentially disruptive issues would remain. One is the relationship between religion and the state. There has always been an important Islamist element in Palestinian nationalism. During the Mandate period, the Muslim religious establishment and Palestinian political leadership were closely intertwined, as epitomized in the dual role of Hajj Amin al-Husayni, the *Mufti* of Jerusalem and head of the Higher Arab Committee. After the debacle of 1948, Hajj Amin presided over the ineffectual Government of All-Palestine based in Gaza, and when that institution was formally dissolved in 1952, he himself declined in importance. But the Muslim Brotherhood, primarily in Egypt, provided a comfortable niche for many Palestinian activists, and some of these —including Yasir 'Arafat—were subsequently instrumental in the formation of explicitly nationalist movements, out of which emerged *Fatah*. Indeed, Muslim solidarity has always been an important impetus to Arab support for the Palestinian cause, beginning with the response to Hajj Amin's convocation of an international Muslim conference in Jerusalem in 1931. And Islamic imagery, ranging from the centrality of Jerusalem to the names (sites of Muslim victories over non-Muslim armies) given to units of the Palestine Liberation Army, has dominated Palestinian political symbolism.[30] Finally, the recent resurgence of Islamic militancy in other parts of the Middle East, aside from producing greater solidarity with the Palestinian cause, has found some expression in Palestinian circles, most notably in the antileftist activities of Muslim fundamentalists in the Gaza Strip, and in the struggle for control of student organizations in West Bank colleges.[31] Thus, the basis for "Muslimist" pressure on issues such as sources of jurisprudence or regulation of private behavior does exist, although its intensity is difficult to gauge.

On the other hand, Palestinian nationalism has always exhibited some secularist tendencies as well. This was partly the result of the prominence of Christian activists in Palestinian politics. Even during the Ottoman period, Christian educators and journalists played a pioneering role in the general Arab cultural revival. In Palestine, Christians like Najib Nasir of Haifa and Isa al-Isa of Jaffa founded newspapers — al-Karmil in 1908 and Filastin in 1911 — that featured vigorous anti-Zionist polemics. Since then, individual Christians have been involved in every stage of Palestinian political action, from the formation of the Muslim-Christian Associations after World War I, in which Christian representation was often disproportionate to their numbers in the population, to the emergence of guerrilla organizations, the most avowedly secularist of which are led by Christians — George Habash of the Popular Front for the Liberation of Palestine (PFLP) and Na'if Hawatma of the Democratic Front for the Liberation of Palestine (DFLP).[32] Christian interest in a confessionally neutral nationalism is self-evident. However, Christian influence on the outcome of a struggle over the religious character of the state would probably be less than decisive. Indeed, excessive Christian activism on any issue except anti-Zionism might be counterproductive, for it could stimulate sectarian atavisms (as the rule of the minority Alawis has apparently done among the Sunni Muslim majority in Syria).

Thus, the major determinant of the state's religious character will be the attitude of the Muslim majority. Most indicators are that this majority would reject both overt secularism and theocracy, and would incline toward a state that is officially Muslim but practically nonintrusive. Aggressive secularism would be too provocative to the sensitivities of Muslims and too radical a departure from both Palestinian tradition and the prevailing practice in the other Arab states, almost all of which have established Islam as the state religion and many of which base their legal systems on Islamic jurisprudence. Even the modernized Palestinian elites, who personally are nonpracticing Muslims and who may hold negative attitudes toward religious functionaries, nevertheless express an appreciation for Islam as a moral guideline, a cultural-historical framework, and a vehicle of community organization, that is, as a valid symbol of collective identity. They can therefore be expected to concur in certain constitutional formulas, public observance of Islamic holidays and customs, state support for — and control of — religious institutions, and so on.[33] However, these same elites, along with other secularized elements, Christians, and ideological "progressives" from the territories or the organizations outside — perhaps even supported by Islamic reformers — could also be expected to resist energetically anything resembling Iranian-style theocracy or the pervasive and oppressive brand of official religion, complete with "morals police," practiced in Saudi Arabia or Libya.

The precise balance between the two tendencies might fluctuate in response to changing tempers, but would probably remain within a fairly narrow spectrum of moderation. Advocates of either extreme are, at the present time at least, relatively few in number, and unless this changes, the religious character of the state should not be a dangerously destabilizing issue.

A more vexatious ideological problem might be the socioeconomic coloration of the regime, that is, the extent to which it is radical or moderate on questions of distributive welfare. The issue is potentially inflammable in two ways: philosophically, as a question of lofty principle; practically, as a struggle for the political and material spoils of sovereignty. Although Palestinian society has always been highly stratified, the distribution of wealth, especially land, was never as highly skewed as in Iraq, Egypt, or, to a lesser extent, in Syria. Furthermore, since the late Ottoman period, when the social hegemony of the great landowning notable families was most pronounced, there was a steady, if uneven, decline in the incidence of rural landlessness and misery. This was partly due to circumstances, such as the availability of alternative sources of employment, unique to, Palestine. But whatever the causes, economic inequality was less extreme in Palestine than in surrounding countries. In the West Bank and Gaza, moreover, there has been a further redistribution of wealth in favor of the lower classes as profitable outlets for surplus labor were found in Transjordan, the oil-producing states, and, most markedly, in Israel after 1967.[34]

In the absence of intolerable inequality, there is no widespread base for extreme egalitarian tendencies. In fact, the nationalist movement as a whole has generally neglected questions of socioeconomic doctrine. Within the occupied territories, members of even the wealthiest families feel no reservations about endorsing the most "radical" political positions; men like Bassam al-Shak'a of Nablus and Karim Khalaf of Ramallah have become their most outspoken advocates. Outside the territories, political fragmentation exists for a number of reasons, but explicit socioeconomic doctrine is not one of them. The conflicts that fracture the PLO are primarily conflicts over the methods and militancy with which the struggle ought to be pursued, or over control of power, rather than over postindependence visions of society. Indeed, distinctive perspectives on the social order are not even implied by the social composition of the various organizations. There is no clear class differentiation among memberships, and although the radical organizations tend to rely more on leftist terminology, it is difficult—at least in the camps —"to distinguish a *Fateh* [*sic*] militant from one from the *Jebha* [PFLP] or the *Democratiyyeh* [DFLP]."[35] Furthermore, the organizations all draw their leadership from the same social stratum, the educated middle class,[36] and the Executive Committee of the PLO even includes some members of the great notable families. A prolonged and divisive class conflict cannot therefore be projected directly from either the social structure of the territories—unless a nationalistically inspired drive for economic autarky were to reverse current sociological trends—or the current ideological preoccupation of the various organizations.

However, it is altogether possible that the very attainment of independence would itself alter conditions significantly. For one thing, latent doctrinal contradictions between the organizations might become overt once the unifying influence of the national struggle is removed. Although class-based ideologies have not yet been fully articulated, the radical organizations do already express their apprehension that a state would provide a mechanism for the domination of the Palestinian "right," and mutual mistrust between the organizations and the bourgeoisie is endemic.[37] Indeed, some Palestinians have argued that national abnormality is a major obstacle to the maturation of class consciousness and that class struggle can, and will, replace nationalist struggle once an independent state is achieved.[38]

Furthermore, independence is likely to alter the structure of society in the West Bank and Gaza. The number of Palestinians immigrating to the new state is a matter of conjecture, but it is reasonable to assume that the desire to move will be strongest precisely among those least well integrated elsewhere, the poor and the unskilled.[39] These immigrants will enhance both the relative size and the expectations of the underprivileged strata, and they are liable to upset whatever measure of social equilibrium now exists, unless their demands can be met by growth rather than by redistribution.

The probability therefore exists that independence, or even the prospect of independence, would activate barely submerged conflicts over the social purpose of the state. Indeed, one argument adduced even now against a West Bank state is precisely the fear that its primary beneficiaries would be Palestinian "politicians, technocrats and merchants," rather than the lower classes and resistance fighters, in whose name the struggle is ostensibly being waged.[40] These conflicts will be expressed in class-based competition over control of the state machinery — that is, the authority to decide policy and allocate resources — and articulated either by existing organizations or by those yet to be consolidated.[41]

There are other potential dimensions of confrontation. One may be a basic tension between the current residents of the West Bank and Gaza and those who would come from outside, including most of the PLO itself. Area residents continually proclaim their loyalty to the PLO, and the organizations have made an effort to maintain links with the territories, to the point where prominent deportees have been coopted into leadership positions. Nevertheless, there is a feeling on the part of some area residents that the PLO is not wholly aware of or sensitive to their concerns and is perhaps more directly representative of Palestinian constituencies elsewhere. The PLO, for its part, has been suspicious of independent initiatives by local activists, fearing that they might evolve into an alternative leadership. These tensions reflect a sense of localism expressed in the argument of the Ramallah lawyer Husayn al-Shuyukhi that the area residents are not a flock of sheep "whose fate should be determined by a man ['Arafat] who does not even own a house in the West Bank and who has no brother in this area so that he can feel what we feel."[42] Compounding this inherent localism might be contradictory claims over credit for the attainment of independence. Outsiders may argue that their political and military efforts created the state; insiders, insisting that their endurance and willingness to stand fast preserved the Arab character of the territories, will resent the large-scale intrusion of others, not alien but not quite native either.[43] Control by outsiders may be forcefully imposed, but the incomplete integration of refugees into local West Bank power structures after 1948 suggests that such control will not be enthusiastically welcomed by the indigenous population, especially by those local elites who may view themselves as natural candidates for the same positions of power and prestige.[44]

A final potential source of political instability is regionalism. Even within this compact territory, subregional attachments already exist. Although the cultural preeminence of Jerusalem is everywhere acknowledged, political domination during the Mandate by Jerusalem (as embodied in the Husayni family) aroused resentment elsewhere, especially in Nablus, which saw itself as a rival source of leadership. When the political status of Jerusalem was consciously diminished in Hashemite policy after 1949, Nablus families were among the main beneficiaries. Similarly, a measure of mutual contempt sometimes characterizes Nablus-Hebron relations; the former is held by some Hebronites to be materialistic and impious, while the latter is occasionally viewed by Nabulsis as backward and provincial.[45]

These attachments, although a legacy of the traditional parochialism that viewed a particular village or town as the true *watan* (homeland), persist as a simple manifestation of local pride. But after independence, they may be intensified by competition for political power or economic advantage. Still, regionalism of this sort underlies the politics of many countries without representing an insuperable obstacle to stability, and it is hardly inconsistent with national cohesiveness.

The problem in a Palestinian state, however, would be further exacerbated by the physical separation of its constituent parts. In terms of their family and educational links, their trading patterns, and perhaps even their political vistas, the West Bank and the Gaza Strip are oriented in opposite directions. Furthermore, central government welfare policy would have a differential impact on the two regions, since per capita income in the Gaza Strip, although rising more rapidly than in the West Bank, remains about 30 percent lower.[46] Nevertheless, other states with similar problems (for example, Prussia before 1871 and the United States today) have demonstrated that centrifugal tendencies are not an inevitable consequence of fragmentation. Only when territorial fragmentation, like regionalism in general, coincides with religious or ethnic cleavage — as in the Dutch revolt against Spain in 1566 or the Bengali revolt against Pakistan in 1971 — does it become a debilitating impediment to political stability. These conditions would not obtain in a Palestinian state. Technically, fragmentation might be awkward, but like the more diffuse problem of regional attachments, it is not necessarily incompatible with the emergence of a reasonably stable political system.

Whether or not all these potential tensions can, in practice, be contained tolerably well will depend on the creation of a political formula and political institutions to legitimize the distribution and exercise of power. Within the West Bank and Gaza, municipal governments and local chambers of commerce have functioned semi-independently for decades. Voluntary agencies and the United Nations Relief and Works Agency (UNRWA) provide a wide range of health, welfare, and educational services to supplement the work of the military government departments (education, health, transportation, commerce, agriculture). Both the social service institutions and the civil affairs administration are staffed by local residents — exclusively in the case of the charitable societies, and at all but the highest levels in the case of UNRWA and the military government. These officials constitute an experienced cadre for the bureaucracy of an independent state.[47] Outside the territories, a bureaucratic infrastructure has emerged in areas under PLO control, especially in the camps in Lebanon, where the Department for Popular Organizations administers a wide range of social, educational-vocational, and public health facilities.[48]

Thus, the challenge of governance, in the sense of administering the state apparatus, will be manageable, since some measure of technical capacity already exists. More serious is the political problem of determining criteria for resource distribution, popular participation, and leadership selection, that is, of determining relations among citizens and between citizens and the state. If some measure of cultural consensus emerges in the form of functioning institutions — a party system, a political "church," or an accepted aristocracy — these questions may be resolved in a fairly stable manner in the postindependence period. Otherwise, they may be decided by force, and it is quite certain that force alone cannot sustain a stable polity for long.

However, even in the unlikely eventuality of permanent instability, the continuing diversionary value of the Israeli issue cannot be simply extrapolated from previous experience in the Arab world. As long as Arab-Israeli relations remain in a state of armed truce, Israel constitutes a visible and convenient object for emotional exploitation by government and opposition alike. In the environment following a peace treaty, some residual hostility will remain, but the immediacy of the conflict will decline and the political return on efforts to manipulate it will probably decline accordingly. Thus, while the prospects for political stability in an independent Palestinian state are not assured, the risk that instability will be of such dimensions and character as to threaten Israeli security does not appear to be great.

Economic challenges to Palestinian stability

A second major obstacle to a Palestinian state's capacity to sustain a nonbelligerent posture may be economic. If the state's inability to satisfy the economic needs of its subjects were so pronounced as to threaten a government's position, that government might feel compelled to renew the confrontation with Israel, either to divert domestic discontent in general, to elicit more Arab economic aid, or, most ambitiously, to secure some specific economic advantage such as arable land, control over water supplies, or Dead Sea mineral resources.

Economic needs cannot be determined a priori. They will be

defined by size of population and subjective expectations. Some fairly arbitrary assumptions about both factors must be made if an assessment of the magnitude of the danger is to be attempted. The state's capacity to satisfy overall needs depends in large part on production factors available, but since these are not confined to domestically generated resources, some assumptions about foreign assistance are also required. It is important to stress, however, that nonviability, that is, the economic threat of an accidental confrontation state, cannot be prejudged solely on the basis of the state's size or natural resources.

It is conceivable, of course, that the euphoria of independence would spill over into other realms, creating unrealistic expectations of the economic millennium. In that case, disillusionment would be swift and destabilizing. However, a more reasonable challenge to the new state would be the minimal expectation that it not entail an economic sacrifice for its inhabitants by reducing their preindependence standard of living. Thus, the economic improvement experienced by large numbers of workers since 1967 would have to be preserved. Furthermore, certain groups—such as managerial and professional workers, civil servants and hotel-keepers—who believe that their economic interests were adversely affected by the Israeli occupation, would expect independence to restore them to their previous status. Finally, Palestinians would probably expect their state to provide economic opportunities at least comparable to those in neighboring states with comparable resources, particularly Jordan.[49]

These fairly modest expectations would tax the capacity of a West Bank/Gaza state, even if they applied only to the current population. Since the annual rate of natural increase in the territories is now about 3.1 percent,[50] real growth of the same magnitude would be required just to prevent deterioration, and more would be needed if the gap with Jordan were to be narrowed.[51] The problem, of course, would be greatly complicated by the immigration of Palestinians from other parts of the Middle East, and that question might therefore be a proper subject of negotiations.

It is impossible to foresee how many Palestinians would

want to move to a West Bank/Gaza state. Much would actually depend on the initial political-economic performance of that state. Spontaneous estimates by Palestinians themselves range from 500,000 to 1,200,000, within as little as one year or as much as fifteen years.[52] Perhaps the most useful approach is to identify those Palestinian constituencies which, because of a combination of push and pull factors, would be most inclined to immigrate to a West Bank/Gaza state.

The most prominent of these are probably those who fled those areas in 1967 and are currently unable to return; they would presumably feel a particular attraction to the West Bank and Gaza in addition to the general allure of an independent state. According to one UNRWA estimate, these people numbered some 250,000 by December 1967, including about 150,000 1948 refugees, for whom the pull factor might be somewhat weaker.[53] If this subgroup increased at the same rate as that of the total refugee population (37 percent since 1967, according to UNRWA), it should have comprised about 342,500 people by 1980, almost all on the East Bank. Of the remaining refugees, about 692,000 (again according to UNRWA statistics) are already in the West Bank and Gaza, leaving a total of about 810,000 — 227,000 in Lebanon, 209,000 in Syria, and about 374,000 in Jordan.

These 810,000 are the bulk of the 1948 refugees, and their fate is primarily a political problem, not an economic one. Nevertheless, the resolution of this problem has important economic ramifications, and if its main thrust is to be resettlement in a Palestinian state in the West Bank and Gaza, then the economic capacity of the state to absorb these refugees is a major determinant of future stability.

Of the refugees now outside the West Bank and Gaza, those in Lebanon would presumably feel the strongest impulse to move. In view of their legal/social marginality and the endemic instability there, these refugees would be more inclined than other 1948 refugees to prefer the prospects of an independent Palestine to their current situation, even if their own family origins are in Israel, rather than the West Bank or Gaza. Those in Syria are in a somewhat different situation. Although they

are officially classified as refugees, they have virtually full
equality, including the right to join the armed forces and the
civil service, and they consequently enjoy a much higher sense
of personal and job security than do those in Lebanon.[54] Given
their lack of particular attachment to the West Bank/Gaza,
most would probably choose to remain in Syria, although
perhaps 60,000 of the least integrated — using camp residence as
a rough indicator[55] — might be considered as candidates for immigration to the new state. In Jordan, the process of integration
has gone furthest. Citizenship has been conferred on all Palestinians, and all legal distinctions have been abolished. For the
refugees resident in Jordan since before 1967, there is no sentimental or economic (as opposed, perhaps, to political) attraction to the West Bank, and therefore no reason to suppose that
they would exchange their present condition for the uncertainty
of life in a Palestinian state. Even for the minority remaining in
camps — about 93,000[56] — the pull of the West Bank, barring
some economic miracle there, would probably remain as weak
as it was before 1967, when westward movement was possible
but virtually nonexistent. On the other hand, there are large
numbers of nonrefugee Palestinians in the East Bank with family
in the West Bank, and some of them (perhaps a few thousand)
might be tempted to reestablish residence there in the aftermath
of independence. Thus, 100,000 may represent the maximum
number of camp dwellers and nonrefugees interested in moving
from the East Bank to the West.

These four constituencies — the 1967 refugees, the refugees in
Lebanon, the camp residents in Syria, and refugees in Jordan
before 1967 — together produce a potential immigrant pool of
about 730,000. In addition, there are Palestinians in other
parts of the world who might be tempted to relocate by the opportunity to play leading professional or administrative roles in
the new state. An estimated 450–500,000 Palestinians reside in
the oil-producing states and, to a lesser extent, in Western
Europe and the Americas. Their personal status is somewhat
ambiguous, especially in Kuwait, where the largest concentration (over 200,000) is found. Nevertheless, most have achieved
a measure of economic and social integration, and would be

reluctant to uproot themselves. Some, however, will be at-
tracted to a Palestinian state for political reasons; others will
feel increasingly insecure as the pressure from indigenous competition for the administrative/clerical positions they now hold
grows. For purposes of this analysis, it is simply assumed that
about 20,000 of these Palestinians would decide, for one reason
or another, to move to the new state. Thus, a reasonable estimate of the maximum number of potential candidates for immigration to the new state is about 750,000.

An immediate influx of this magnitude would surely over-
whelm the absorptive capacity of the new state. Some of their
needs — food, shelter, education for their children — would have
to be satisfied immediately in order to avoid politically dangerous unrest. And their complete economic rehabilitation
could not be prolonged indefinitely, since an outstanding refugee problem, which this process of repatriation is intended to
eliminate, would constitute a continuing source of instability in
the region. Therefore, a phased process of absorption, lasting
perhaps five years, would seem to be a reasonable response to
the political and practical imperatives.[57]

Since this process would begin after the conclusion of a peace
settlement, the economic exigencies would depend on the actual
circumstances prevailing at the time. A projection of requirements can be made from data for 1980, the last year for which
complete information is available, but it would yield results for
the period 1981–1985 that are already obsolete and cannot,
therefore, be used for predictive or operational purposes. For
purposes of illustration, however, it can be imagined that the
transition period had begun in 1981, in which case over 800,000
people (allowing for annual natural increase of about 2.5
percent[58]) would move to the new state during the transition. If
the absolute number of immigrants were held constant over the
five years (see table 1), then the economic pressures would be
greatest at the very beginning, when the new state was least
equipped to cope with the attendant demands. If, instead, the
immigration were controlled in such a way as to produce constant proportional population increase (see table 2), then the annual growth over the five years would be about 10.77 percent,

Table 1. Projected population change in a Palestinian state, 1981-1985, assuming constant absolute decrease in immigrant pool abroad (in thousands).

	1981	1982	1983	1984	1985
Potential immigrants abroad					
at beginning of year	750.0	607.4	461.1	311.2	157.5
Natural increase (at 2.5%)	18.8	15.1	11.5	7.7	3.9
Immigrants during year	161.4	161.4	161.4	161.4	161.4
Year-end immigrant pool	607.4	461.1	311.2	157.5	0.0
Percent decrease during year	19.0	24.1	32.5	49.4	100.0
Population of West Bank/Gaza					
at beginning of year	1145.9	1342.8	1545.8	1755.1	1970.9
Natural increase (at 3.1%)	35.5	41.6	47.9	54.4	61.1
Immigrants during year	161.4	161.4	161.4	161.4	161.4
Year-end population	1342.8	1545.8	1755.1	1970.9	2193.4
Percent increase during year	17.2	15.1	13.5	12.3	11.3

necessitating an overall economic growth rate of approximately 13.87 percent per year merely to maintain current per capita income levels. Furthermore, maintaining full employment at the current labor force participation rate of 18.7 percent of the population — a low rate, explained by the age structure of the population as well as the traditional bias against female employment outside the home — would require the generation of an additional 195,000 jobs by the end of the transition period.[59] Housing, education, transportation, and health facilities would also have to grow substantially just to meet the assumed minimal expectation levels.[60]

A Palestinian state would be hard-pressed to satisfy these economic needs. The scarcity of natural resources and a restricted domestic market would severely limit the potential for self-sustained growth in the West Bank and Gaza. The problem would be further exacerbated if a Palestinian state decided, either as a "nonbelligerent" expression of residual hostility or as

Table 2. Projected population change in a Palestinian state, 1981–1985, assuming constant proportional increase (in thousands).

	1981	1982	1983	1984	1985
Potential immigrants abroad					
at beginning of year	750.0	645.4	521.3	374.6	202.0
Natural increase (at 2.5%)	18.8	16.3	13.2	9.5	5.1
Immigrants during year	123.4	140.4	159.9	182.1	207.1[a]
Year-end immigrant pool	645.4	521.3	374.6	202.0	0.0
Percent decrease during year	13.95	19.23	28.14	46.08	100.0
Population of West Bank/Gaza					
at beginning of year	1145.9	1304.8	1485.7	1691.7	1926.3
Natural increase (at 3.1%)	35.5	40.5	46.1	52.5	59.8
Immigrants during year	123.4	140.4	159.9	182.1	207.3[a]
Year-end population	1304.8	1485.7	1691.7	1926.3	2193.4
Percent increase during year	13.87	13.87	13.87	13.87	13.87

a. These two figures do not equal because of rounding.

part of a more general posture of economic nationalism, to curtail economic links with Israel. Established trade patterns would be disrupted and some Israeli markets would be closed to Palestinian suppliers.[61] But the most severe effects would be felt in the labor market.

Since 1968, employment in Israel has provided the main engine for the impressive economic growth that has taken place in the occupied territories. By 1980, some 72,000 West Bank and Gaza residents, according to a survey of the labor force, were working in Israel.[62] In that year, these workers constituted almost 35 percent of the total labor force of the territories, including those self-employed, and almost 57 percent of all employees (see table 3). Their wages contributed almost one-sixth of combined GNP in the two areas (see table 4).

If access to the Israeli labor market were suddenly closed off, the economic impact would be disastrous, in Gaza even more than in the West Bank. The direct effects could be some-

Table 3. Labor force characteristics in the West Bank/ Gaza, 1980 (in thousands).

	West Bank	Gaza	Total
Total employed[a]	131.2	79.4	210.6
Employed in Israel	38.4	33.5	71.9
As percent of total employed	29.3	42.2	34.1
Total employees	73.0	50.7	123.7
Employees in Israel	37.3	33.1	70.4
As percent of total employees	51.1	65.3	56.9

Source: Computed from *Statistical Abstract of Israel*, no. 32 (1981), tables xxvii/19, p. 732, xxvii/20, p. 733, and xxvii/22, p. 736.

a. Including self-employed.

Table 4. Sources of income in the West Bank/Gaza, 1980 (Israeli shekels, millions).[a]

	West Bank	Gaza	Total
GNP at factor cost	5192.9	2145.7	7338.6
Total wages from abroad	1015.8	701.2	1717.0
Wages from Israel[b]	711.1	490.8	1201.9
Wages from Israel as percent of GNP	13.7	22.9	16.4

Source: My calculations from *Statistical Abstract of Israel*, no. 32 (1981), tables xxvii/6, pp. 716–717, and xxvii/10, p. 720.

a. In 1980, Israeli currency was changed, and the shekel replaced the pound at a rate of 1:10. The average exchange rate in U.S. funds was I.S. = $0.18.

b. Calculated at 70 percent of total wages from abroad, using estimate given in Israel, Central Bureau of Statistics, *Administered Territories Statistics Quarterly*, 10 (December 1980), p. 80.

what mitigated in the short-run by international welfare payments. Still, the distortions in the labor market would be severe and the social-psychological costs would be debilitating. The ensuing disruption of class relations — given that the major burden of adjustment would fall on the unskilled and semi-skilled laborers rather than on owners of land or capital — would undoubtedly be reflected in domestic politics.

Given the staggering economic difficulties of absorbing both repatriates from abroad and workers from Israel, it is rather unlikely that Palestinian authorities would initiate an immediate and complete severance of economic ties with Israel. In this regard, the precedent established by Algerian governments with respect to postindependence relations with France may be instructive. However, even a gradual, selective, and well-managed decoupling from Israel, which permitted some continuing labor mobility, would leave the Palestinian state with a formidable problem of meeting, on its own, the economic challenges it is likely to face.

For the fundamental fact remains that the West Bank and Gaza are small, poorly endowed in natural resources, and unable to sustain the kind of domestic market that makes economies of scale possible. Poor resource-to-population ratios have always been reflected in negative migration balances. Significant emigration from these areas was evident even during the late Ottoman period, when improved public security made movement into the coastal plain more attractive; more psychically mobile Christians from Ramallah and Bethlehem sought relief from economic constraints in places as remote as North and South America. During the British Mandate, when the overall Arab migration balance was positive, population growth in most of the West Bank was still much lower than the national average, indicating a large internal migration toward the coast and Jerusalem. After 1949, the population flow shifted eastward, as an estimated 300,000 West Bank residents pursued economic opportunities in Transjordan or other parts of the eastern Arab world.[63] And even though the general economic situation has improved since 1968, perhaps 150,000 Palestinians have still left the territories, some of them students, but many of them workers, including a high proportion of professionals and managerial or technical workers, looking, temporarily or permanently, for better prospects elsewhere.[64]

The basic factors that limited economic potential in the past would continue to constrain the growth potential of a Palestinian state in the future. Land area is small — about 5,870,000 dunams in the West Bank and Gaza. Of this, only about 1,800,000 are currently cultivated — 1,608,000 in the West Bank and approximately 200,000 in Gaza.[65] Gaza, furthermore, is already overexploiting its water sources by approximately 40–50 million cubic meters a year. The West Bank does have a potential surplus of 630–775 million cubic meters, but tapping this surplus would require extensive investment and drawing on the western subterranean aquifer which straddles the border between the West Bank and Israel.[66] Mineral resources are nonexistent; building materials — except for stone — are scarce; and there are no domestic energy sources.

However, growth potential is not strictly limited by these factors, Even now, some resources are underexploited. In the West Bank, for example, some 150,000 dunams have gone out of production since the early 1970s,[67] and according to one estimate, as much as 250,000 more are potentially cultivable.[68] West Bank water reserves, as noted above, are substantial; in the Gaza Strip, existing reserves could be used more efficiently, and more water for irrigation could be made available through sharing agreements with the West Bank and Israel, through desalination, or, as a long-term solution, through access to Nile Valley water from Egypt.[69] Skilled technical manpower, unlike unskilled labor on the one hand and high-level professional manpower on the other, is not in great abundance,[70] but there are now about 5,325 students undergoing vocational training in the West Bank and Gaza — 1,325 in UNRWA facilities and 4,000 in government training centers — and over 42,000 have passed through the latter since 1968.[71] Although many of these graduates are now outside the country, they could, together with future trainees and others who gained experience in Israeli industry, provide much of the manpower needed to apply more advanced production techniques in all sectors of an independent economy.

Thus, the major short-term variable determining actual growth rates would appear to be investment capital. Capital requirements for the transition period are extremely difficult to foresee. The relationship between investment and growth is unclear, and the ability of the current infrastructure to absorb the necessary amounts is not self-evident. However, a very rough order of magnitude may be suggested by the data in table 5, which would be generated if the five-year transition period had been 1981–1985. These data are based on the following assumptions:

- population and GNP grow at a rate of 13.87 percent per annum;
- GNP per capita remains at the 1980 level of $1158;
- net factor payments from abroad, mostly wages from Israel, remain unchanged at their current level, that is, about $329.7 million in constant 1980 dollars;
- the import surplus as a proportion of GNP remains constant at 1980 levels, that is, 35.9 percent;
- private consumption and government consumption grow in direct proportion to GNP, that is, at 13.87 percent per annum.

The projected investment needs for the five-year period — about $3.3 billion — is only a very crude approximation. A more reliable projection would require a detailed sector analysis. Furthermore, the projection may err on the side of understatement, since it depends on assumptions of minimal expectations, especially concerning constant per capita GNP, which may be overly optimistic. However, other analyses have produced capital requirements of similar magnitude. One survey of manpower needs, for example, concluded that about $3.5 billion (in 1975 prices) would be needed over a five-year period to produce a sound employment structure for an economy integrating about twice as many repatriates as have been assumed here.[72]

Thus, $3.3 billion would seem to be a not unreasonable working estimate. Capital of this magnitude could be generated by a variety of sources. Surprisingly, one important source might be domestic savings, which have not been fully exploited in the past. From 1975 to 1980, real gross domestic product, which discounts the direct effect of income earned abroad, grew

Table 5. Projected national accounts of a Palestinian state in a transition period, 1981–1985 ($ million, 1980 prices).

	1980 (actual)[a]	1981	1982	1983	1984	1985	1981–85 (total)
Gross national product	1326.7	1510.7	1720.2	1958.7	2230.4	2539.7	—
Less net factor payments	329.7	329.7	329.7	329.7	329.7	329.7	—
Gross domestic product	997.0	1181.0	1390.5	1629.0	1900.7	2210.0	—
Plus import surplus	476.0	524.0	617.2	702.8	800.2	911.2	—
Total resources	1473.0	1723.0	2007.7	2331.8	2700.9	3111.2	—
Less private consumption	1032.3	1175.5	1338.5	1524.1	1735.5	1976.1	—
Less government consumption	109.9	125.1	142.5	162.3	184.8	210.4	—
Required investment	330.8	422.4	526.7	645.4	780.6	924.7	3299.8

a. *Statistical Abstract of Israel*, no. 32 (1981), table xxvii/6, pp. 716–717 (at exchange rate of $1 = I.S.5.64, computed from data in table ix/11, p. 238).

at a combined average annual rate of about 8.9 percent (slightly higher in the West Bank, lower in Gaza). While some of this may be attributed to the indirect effects of economic integration with Israel, for example, access to larger markets, most is apparently the fruit of domestic capital formation, almost 90 percent of which was private. In the same six-year period, private investment, which amounted to almost 18 percent of private disposable income, grew at an average annual rate of about 8.5 percent. However, a very high proportion of this investment — almost 70 percent in 1980 — has gone into residential housing, rather than into buildings, machinery, or equipment that could stimulate subsequent growth. Furthermore, a very considerable portion of savings has not been invested domestically at all, but has been hoarded — in foreign currency or gold — or sent abroad, especially to the East Bank. This phenomenon was particularly pronounced before the 1973 war, but even in the period 1975–1980, imputed savings (private disposable income less private consumption) exceeded private domestic investment by an average yearly rate of about 12 percent. Failure to invest up to the theoretical maximum resulted from a number of factors: political uncertainty, reluctance to use the Israeli banking system, and vestiges of the inclination to hoard typically found in traditional societies.[73]

Much of this shut-in investment capacity could presumably be exploited in an independent state, either by the reduction of political uncertainty and the creation of an indigenous credit system and capital market, or, perhaps less efficiently, by a central government prepared to borrow or tax away hoarded savings and direct them to more productive uses. In either case, commitment of unused savings could leave current consumption patterns unchanged, while increasing total investment by almost 10 percent per year over prevailing levels. But even if some hoarding continued, because of initial uncertainty or the persistent force of tradition, domestic capital invested (assuming that the savings-rate remained constant at about 25.5 percent of private consumption expenditure) would still amount to almost $1.8 billion (see table 6). Thus, domestic investment could make a major contribution to economic growth.

Table 6. Investment capital required in a Palestinian state during a transition period, 1981–1985, and possible sources ($ million, 1980 prices).

	1981	1982	1983	1984	1985	Total
Capital required[a]	422.4	526.7	645.4	780.6	924.7	3299.8
Possible sources:						
Domestic savings	299.8	341.3	388.6	442.6	503.9	1976.2
(less 10% hoarding)	30.0	34.1	38.9	44.3	50.4	197.7
Domestic sources	269.8	307.2	349.7	398.3	453.5	1778.5
UN assistance program[b]	0.0	18.4	40.2	66.1	96.5	221.2
Total	269.8	325.6	389.9	464.4	550.0	1999.7
Balance required from other						
sources	152.6	201.1	255.5	316.2	374.7	1300.1

a. From table 5.
b. From table 7.

However, it is precisely in the early years of the state's independence that private investor confidence, rather than growing, might actually be reduced, and imported institutional capital (from American and Arab governments and multinational sources) would clearly be needed, both as a political signal and to finance the additional growth required to satisfy assumed expectations. The availability of imported capital would itself be subject to political considerations. Theoretically, however, the money could easily be secured from funds already allocated to the Palestinian cause, including those by international organizations such as UNRWA. Because its continued existence would symbolically perpetuate a refugee issue that the peace settlement is intended to eliminate, UNRWA should be abolished simultaneously with the achievement of a settlement and its personnel assigned to the Palestinian government or to voluntary organizations. UNRWA funds should be transferred to a five-year UN Assistance Program for Palestine, preferably within an existing framework such as the UN Development Program.

An appropriate portion of the $211.3 million spent by UNRWA in 1980 – about 37.5 percent, corresponding to UNRWA's estimate of the proportion of refugees already in the West Bank and Gaza – should be made immediately available to the new Palestinian government for refugee rehabilitation.[74] The remainder – less an amount based on current UNRWA budgets to maintain those potential immigrants as yet unrepatriated – could be released to the Palestinian government at prescribed intervals. (It is assumed that Palestinians outside the West Bank and Gaza opting not to move to the new state would become citizens of other states, or at least permanent residents holding Palestinian citizenship. In any event, they would cease to be the responsibility of international organizations.) If population transfer is effected according to the rates suggested in table 2, the funds available for investment, after resettlement of current-year immigrants is financed, would amount to some $221.2 million over the five-year period (see table 7).

Table 7. Capital from proposed UN assistance program for Palestine (using UNRWA funds, $ million, 1980 prices).

	1981	1982	1983	1984	1985	Total
Total program budget	211.3	211.3	211.3	211.3	211.3	1056.5
Less current allocation to West Bank/Gaza[a]	79.2	79.2	79.2	79.2	79.2	396.0
Current allocation outside West Bank/Gaza	132.1	132.1	132.1	132.1	132.1	660.5
Less maintenance of remaining unrepatriated refugees[b]	110.9	89.6	64.4	34.7	0.0	299.6
Less maintenance cost for current-year repatriates[b]	21.2	24.1	27.5	31.3	35.6	139.7
Available for investment	0.0	18.4	40.2	66.1	96.5	221.2

a. For rehabilitation of in-place refugees and arriving immigrants.
b. At $171.8 per capita, based on 1980 UNRWA budget.

The capital shortfall to be secured from other sources would therefore be approximately $1300 million, or about $260 million per year. In view of the financial support already given for the Palestine cause by benefactors other than the United Nations, this should not be a difficult sum to raise. The Baghdad Summit Conference in 1978, for example, pledged (but probably did not fully deliver) $250 million per year to the PLO, and gross revenues of the PLO—from Arab aid, taxation of Palestinians abroad, and income from a variety of other activities (including legitimate business enterprises)—has been estimated as high as $500 million per year.[75] Even if the capital requirement were double that indicated here, Arab oil producers interested in preventing economically induced instability in a Palestinian state (and, not incidentally, minimizing that state's dependence on radical or non-Arab forces) could easily supply the necessary funds. Furthermore, the United States and other industrial nations would presumably be prepared to participate in bilateral or multilateral assistance programs if they were necessary to consolidate a political settlement.

Indeed, the small scale of the Palestinian economy might mean that the initial limiting factor on growth would actually be, not a shortage of capital, but rather the capacity of the new state to absorb effectively the capital which would be available. According to one analysis, even a government fully committed to economic development could, because of the relatively underdeveloped infrastructure of the West Bank/Gaza, use no more than about $150 million per year in foreign assistance for development purposes.[76]

It should be emphasized that the preceding analysis is based on virtually worst-case economic assumptions. Population pressures, for example, are projected largely from UNRWA estimates on refugees, which are considerably inflated. In 1980, UNRWA reported a total of about 692,000 registered refugees in the West Bank and Gaza. But the Israeli on-site census in 1967 revealed a total of about 322,000 individuals in self-declared refugee families, including those in East Jerusalem. If this figure were extrapolated to 1980 on the basis of the prevailing 3.1 percent per year rate of natural increase in the territories (a rate which ignores emigration and is also higher than that of refugees elsewhere), the result would still be no more than 479,000, about two-thirds of the UNRWA figure. Clearly, the more the Israeli figure reflects the true state of affairs, the more a projection of potential immigration based on UNRWA figures exaggerates the population pressures, and hence, the anticipated economic difficulties.

The projection here also assumes that all of those in the specified constituencies actually would exercise their right to migrate to the new state. This assumption is probably unfounded, especially with respect to Palestinians in Jordan, who would be able to maintain close ties with relatives and business associates in the West Bank without changing their current place of residence.

Furthermore, not all those who did move to the new state would constitute an economic burden on it. Most of the non-refugees, and many of the refugees as well, would bring with them capital, experience, and useful skills. This would be true, a fortiori, of migrants not belonging to the constituencies designated here.

Finally, the economic rehabilitation (as opposed to the social and political integration) of the camp residents already living in the West Bank and Gaza would not present a difficult prior obstacle to be overcome. Over the years, these camps have evolved from their initially wretched state to the point where living conditions in them, while hardly attractive, nevertheless do not fall far below those of established villages and towns. Congestion in the camps is obviously greater, but indicators such as housing density and possession of durable goods show virtually no disparity between the camps and regular settlements.[77]

The economic challenges to the Palestinian state described here are probably greater than those that would actually be encountered because of the assumptions built into this analysis. Yet even these pessimistic assumptions permit relatively sanguine conclusions.

All this notwithstanding, it is still possible that the economic performance of a Palestinian state might fail to satisfy completely expected demands, but the failures would then stem from human choice rather than from inexorable circumstance. Inefficient planning and administration or counterproductive political decisions, such as nationalistically-inspired limitations on economic ties with Israel, might contribute to such an outcome. Economic expectations might also be unrealistically high.

At this level of analysis, however, the entire economic issue becomes, if not altogether irrelevant, then of decidedly secondary importance. For if the minimal requirements (phased absorption of immigrants, some measure of labor mobility, Arab and international assistance) were provided for in a settlement, then postindependence economic performance would become a question of marginal successes or failures, rather than one of basic ability to sustain a society. Nor would these relative successes or failures necessarily be correlated perfectly with political stability. Some measure of unemployment, for example, would quite probably produce the responses characteristic even now of other Mediterranean countries — emigration or the temporary export of labor — rather than political upheaval.

It may be true that balanced economic growth would provide a more auspicious environment for domestic politics, and large-scale international assistance for such growth is therefore important. A direct economic stake for Palestine in peaceful relations with Israel would almost certainly enhance the possibility and durability of such relations, and economic cooperation — perhaps including joint ventures — should also be encouraged. But unless foreign support is totally absent (as opposed to less-than-optimal), and unless oil revenues diminish to the point where Arab sources of capital and outlets for surplus Palestinian labor are altogether eliminated, the probability of an economic situation so desperate as to make domestic stability and nonbelligerent relations with Israel impossible is quite low.

Historically, both the viability of states and the quality of their relations with other states have been determined more by political and strategic factors than by questions of economic existence. The evidence seems to suggest that this would probably be true in the case of a Palestinian state as well.

Palestine as an enlisted confrontation state

The analysis of potential threats to stability has concentrated thus far on possible ideological or systemic challenges from within the Palestinian state itself. Another source of concern stems from regional or international dynamics, and specifically from the possibility that radical Arab states or the Soviet Union might find in the Palestinian state a useful vehicle for the promotion of their own influence or presence in this part of the Middle East, either in the Arab-Israeli or inter-Arab arenas.

With respect to the Arab-Israeli arena, this danger does not require that radical Arab or Soviet leaders be more hostile to Israel than the leaders of a Palestinian state itself, although in some cases (as in that of Muammar al-Qadhdhafi, for example) this may well be true. It only requires the existence of potential opportunities for destabilization that could be exploited by these leaders with the political, economic, or military instruments at their disposal. In other words, it requires either dissident forces within the Palestinian state, a Palestinian government that is coercible, or a Palestinian government itself inclined to pursue a belligerent policy but constrained from doing so and searching for relief from its constraints.

The susceptibility of a Palestinian state to conventional foreign policy pressures at the hands of other states is an unexceptional problem of analysis. However, a word about the issue of enlistment through subversion is in order. That there will be political opposition in a Palestinian state is a virtual certainty —not just by rejectionists on the question of peace with Israel, but by dissidents on the whole gamut of internal and external issues. The ability of outside actors to support these dissidents will depend to some extent on the inherent strength of the latter, an estimation of which has already been attempted.[78] It will also depend on the political permeability of the new state's borders. This will be particularly relevant insofar as other Arab states are concerned.

The theory of Arab nationalism in some sense justifies the active involvement of Arab states in each other's internal politics —either through direct appeals to the public or through more clandestine means such as financial subventions, subornation or infiltration of agents, and provision of weapons and training. With the passage of time, the growing legitimacy of the individual Arab states and the maturation of the state machinery has tended to limit the effectiveness of such practices.[79] This has not, however, ended inter-Arab competition for power and prestige in the region; and in that competition, attempts to penetrate the political systems of other Arab states remain an important weapon. Some states, by virtue of their small size, economic dependence, or delicate internal balance, are more vulnerable to external penetration than others. It is quite probable that a Palestinian state, because of the established ties of different organizations with various Arab regimes, the geographical location and likely economic exigencies, and its very newness, will belong in this category of relatively permeable entities. The Palestinian state's internal politics and foreign policy will therefore be affected, to some extent, by the relative penetration capacities of contending Arab forces.

For reasons already discussed, those states most inclined, whether for ideological or opportunistic reasons, to encourage Palestinian dissidents and attack the Palestinian government on the issue of relations with Israel are precisely those liable to have the least capacity either to coerce or to overthrow a Palestinian government. Libya, and perhaps Iraq (or even Iran), although wealthy, would be financially dispensable. Their physical distance partially immunizes them from the direct costs of renewed Arab-Israeli conflict and therefore encourages a provocative posture, but it would also reduce their access to the Palestinian system and undermine the confidence of a potential Palestinian partner in their ability to deal with the possible consequences of such a posture. On the other hand, those states with the greatest capacity to influence Palestinian politics would probably be impelled by self-interest — on the question of Israel in particular, and indeed, on radicalism in general — not only to resist Palestinian incitement and refrain from exploiting Palestinian grievances, but also to practice active restraint. About Syria, there is, again, greater uncertainty. But its capacity to discomfort a nonbelligerent Palestinian regime would be considerable, and the importance of securing Syrian self-restraint and even Syrian support for measures to eliminate the political-military infrastructure of Palestinian rejectionists, who might attempt to secure sanctuary outside the direct reach of the Palestinian authorities, merely underscores the desirability of involving Syria in the peace process.

The question of Soviet enlistment of a Palestinian state is somewhat different. Unlike most of the Arab states, the Soviet Union, despite its support for the PLO, has explicitly refused even a pro forma endorsement of the PLO's definition of the proper solution to the conflict. Instead, the Soviets have repeatedly affirmed UN Security Council Resolution 242 and insisted on Israel's right to exist within the 1949 borders, thereby signifying that Palestinian territorial aspirations should be confined to the West Bank and Gaza.[80] Furthermore, while they are hardly ardent exponents of Zionism, the Soviets do not share the emotional hostility to Israel of the Palestinians or even other Arabs. Nevertheless, Soviet policy is not governed by sentiment. If the Soviets believed that by stimulating Palestinian instability or tension with Israel — by raising the issue of the 1947 UN Partition Proposal, for example — they could safely advance their own objectives in the region, including the disruption of an "American peace," there is no reason to believe that they would refrain from doing so. If a prowestern Palestinian government, for example, could be either seduced or overthrown as a result of revived conflict with Israel, Soviet efforts to promote such a process could not be excluded.

The magnitude of this threat, however, ought to be examined with reference to probable Soviet motivations and calculations. From the Soviet point of view, the advisability of attempting to enlist a Palestinian state by means of anti-Israel incitement is not self-evident. It is true that a wide range of domestic social and ideological grievances might provide opportunities for Soviet entrée into the Palestinian political system, facilitated by avowedly Marxist-Leninist guerrilla organizations like the Democratic Front for the Liberation of Palestine or, perhaps more reliably, by a local Communist party. Although the Soviet penetration capacity, compared to that of the leading

Arab states, would be handicapped by physical and cultural distance, Palestinian Communists, using popular front tactics, might nevertheless be able to create a receptive environment in the new state for a large Soviet presence. Though relatively few in number, Communists are already fairly well positioned to play a potentially influential role because of the organizational efforts of the Palestine National Front.

The PNF was created in 1972, after the Communist-sponsored guerrilla movement *Quwwat al-Ansar* was disbanded for lack of operational success. Although it was presented as a non-party national movement formed to carry out the work of the PLO inside the occupied territories (and had three representatives elected to the PLO Executive Committee at the thirteenth session of the Palestine National Council in 1977), the PNF has been dominated by Communist activists and maintains a separate organizational existence.[81] It is therefore not coincidental that the PNF receives special attention in the Soviet media, to the point where it, not the PLO, is described as the most authoritative and widely accepted political force among Palestinians inside the occupied territories.[82] Indeed, it is the potential challenge of the PNF to the mainstream of the PLO that may explain the decision of the fifteenth session of the Palestine National Council in 1981 to reduce PNF representation on the Executive Committee to one seat.[83] In short, subversion of a Palestinian state, while hardly inevitable, is not altogether inconceivable; for the Soviets, this would be a considerable achievement entailing relatively few risks.

A large Soviet presence would be a serious matter to many states in the region and elsewhere, but it would not constitute a direct military danger to Israel — unless Soviet hostility to the Jewish state is viewed as teleological and not merely instrumental. And even if the Soviets were committed to the reduction of Israel as an end in itself, their willingness to pursue that objective with their own forces would depend on their perceptions of probable costs and risks, including the risk of American counteraction. Given a credible American deterrent, control of a Palestinian state would not be sufficient for Soviet purposes; without an American deterrent, control of a Palestinian state would not be necessary. From Israel's perspective, the direct Soviet threat would be heightened by the addition of a Soviet presence — in the West Bank and Gaza — to the existing presence in Syria, but it would not constitute a qualitatively new problem. And given the size and quality of Israel's army, a Soviet effort to avoid superpower confrontation by employing proxy forces (for example, Cubans) would be complicated by the difficulty of finding them in numbers sufficient to overturn the regional military balance.

The more probable danger for Israel, then, is of Soviet incitement of regional conflict in order to facilitate less cataclysmic aspirations. Soviet performance in much of the postindependence Third World suggests that the Soviet Union has a comparative advantage over its superpower rival — if at all — as a provider of politicomilitary support, rather than as an ideological inspiration, a cultural or developmental role model, or a source of economic assistance. Therefore, a measure of tension in Palestinian relations with neighboring states would certainly enhance the ability of the Soviets to establish an additional presence in the region.

However, the manipulability of the Arab-Israeli conflict for such purposes cannot be projected on the basis of previous experience. Issues of dispute would inevitably arise, but the instant and automatic incitement value of an anti-Israel posture, which has so often served Soviet purposes in the Arab world in the past, would almost certainly have depreciated as a result of a peace to which the Palestinians themselves had voluntarily agreed.

The benefits to the Soviets of a provocative policy would therefore be limited, not only in the Palestinian state itself, but also, more critically, in other, more strategically attractive Arab states — which would undoubtedly be the ultimate object of the Soviet exercise. For once the Palestinian cause were normalized through the creation of a state, it would lose much of its sanctity as a pan-Arab issue. Other Arab states, especially those closest to Israel, would be able to justify divergent policies grounded in divergent interests, and to resist active involvement in irredentist campaigns for the benefit of a Palestinian state, even if cloaked in the verbiage of Arab rights — as they do now with respect to Iraqi claims against Iran, not to speak of Syrian claims on Hatay province in Turkey — and to dispense with Soviet military support. Thus, the rewards of an anti-Israel campaign would probably be even less substantial than the not-altogether satisfactory benefits of the current Soviet approach.

In view of these somewhat dubious prospects, the potential risks of provocation would surely weigh heavily on the minds of Soviet decisionmakers. For even if they were successful in enlisting the Palestinian state into a confrontationist posture, the consequences could be very dangerous. Without effective control over Palestinian (or Israeli) conduct, the Soviets would have no assurance that a manageable and profitable state of political tension might not be unhinged by some misperception or miscalculation and quickly metastasize into full-fledged military hostilities. In the event that Israel alone retained a military superiority over Palestine alone (and the imbalance of resources together with the provisions of the settlement would virtually ensure that), the Soviets would then be faced with the painful dilemma of either leaving their client to its fate, with the inevitable loss of position there and reputation elsewhere, or intervening militarily on a scale large enough to affect the outcome, thus running a high risk of direct confrontation with the United States over an asset which, in Soviet eyes, could hardly be more than marginal. A probabilistic cost-benefit calculation therefore suggests that the Soviet Union would be unlikely to embark on such a course without some very strong inhibitions.

A different type of destabilization process may involve actions by radical Arab or Soviet decisionmakers that would permit an otherwise-constrained Palestinian state to pursue its own revisionist inclinations. This is not strictly a matter of hostile third parties enlisting an essentially nonbelligerent Palestinian state, but more a question of the situational probability of a purposeful confrontationist state, and since this question has already been treated, it does not require further elaboration, at least with respect to inter-Arab dynamics. The possible role of the Soviet Union, however, merits some consideration.

Soviet willingness to be enlisted by a Palestinian state in an anti-Israel campaign would presumably be governed by the same factors determining its willingness to provoke such a campaign. For regardless of the armory that the Soviet Union might supply, direct participation would almost certainly be required to provide that state with a viable conventional military option. For fairly straightforward reasons just discussed, the Soviets are likely to avoid military entanglement with Israel in the foreseeable circumstances.

A somewhat less risky, hence more plausible, Soviet posture would be to agree to furnish a limited "defensive" umbrella to a Palestinian state. A Soviet military force, in place, might serve to deter massive Israeli reaction to terrorism or sabotage emanating from the Palestinian state; proxy forces would not, since Israel would not be inhibited from clashing with them. A Soviet commitment of this sort, by appearing to increase the Palestinian margin of safety, might very well provoke continuing low-level tension and instability, thus enhancing Palestinian dependence on Soviet protection and entrenching the Soviet position in the new state. Apart from the danger of loss of control — which is not to be dismissed lightly — such a situation would serve Soviet interests well (although its value to a Palestinian regime — aside from emotional release — is somewhat obscure) and is therefore probably the most tangible aspect of the Soviet threat from Israel's perspective.

A situation in which Palestinians could wage sublimited war without fear of large-scale preventive or punitive counteraction would not constitute a mortal danger to Israel's basic security, but it could mean heavy costs in Israeli life and property and would be totally intolerable. It is therefore imperative that the peace agreement include political provisions, such as binding neutrality for the Palestinian state, that would minimize the danger of sublimited war attributable to Soviet policy — this, in addition to the economic and military measures needed to deal with the potential problem of terrorism in general.

Of course, without an American commitment to help restrain Soviet adventurism in the region, such provisions alone would be no real guarantee against Soviet or Soviet-supported threats associated with a Palestinian state. But that would be true, as well, of any other regional configuration, including the present one, and the creation of a Palestinian state, insofar as the magnitude of the Soviet threat to Israel is concerned, would therefore have a minimal impact. Even with an American commitment, the problem would not be completely eliminated, but it would — in the proposed political context — be reduced to manageable proportions.

5

Potential Implications
for Other Israeli Interests

Aside from the potential security threats to Israel, other Israeli interests may be adversely affected by the creation of an independent Palestinian state, even if that state remains nonbelligerent. Independence in the West Bank and Gaza might stimulate secessionist sentiments among Israeli Arabs, thus threatening the integrity even of an Israel reduced to the 1949 armistice lines. Israel's ability to implement its settlement policies and realize its own vision of Jerusalem's future would almost certainly be constrained. And Palestinian economic development — regardless of political motivations — might have a detrimental impact on Israeli access to markets, manpower, and resources.

Of these potential risks, only the first is specifically related to the substantive nature of a Palestinian state in the West Bank and Gaza. The others are more direct consequences of Israeli withdrawal or the loss of Israel's freedom to determine the use of West Bank/Gaza resources, and therefore inhere, in equal measure, in any other likely peace settlement. Nevertheless, a full appreciation of the implications of this particular outcome requires that all these issues be addressed.

The effect on Israeli Arabs

Of all the possible effects specifically attributable to the political (as opposed to territorial) character of a peace settlement, the effect on Jewish-Arab relations within Israel itself is likely to be most profound. Of greatest concern is the possibility that an independent Palestinian state will act as a magnet for the political loyalties of Israeli Arabs, perhaps stimulating demands that heavily Arab-populated parts of Israel be attached to the Palestinian state. The threat of secessionism is in fact one of the gravest implications for Israel of a Palestinian state.

At the end of 1980, the non-Jewish population of Israel (almost all Arabs), amounted to 639,000, or 16.3 percent of the total Israeli population.[1] This proportion had risen from 14.1 percent at the end of 1967 (after the annexation of East Jerusalem), and is likely to continue to rise in the future, barring some massive wave of Jewish immigration, given the much higher rate of natural increase in the the non-Jewish population.[2] Of even greater political salience is the fact that the Arab population is concentrated in a few areas where they actually constitute a majority. It is in these areas — the inland regions of Acre subdistrict, the western half of the Yezre'el subdistrict, and the eastern half of Hadera subdistrict (Wadi 'Ara) — that any Arab irredenta would most likely emerge, especially since the demographic reality could find a quasi-legal rationale in the 1947 UN Partition Plan, which allotted these areas to the Arab state.

Secessionist movements in these areas would represent an intolerable challenge to Israel's territorial integrity and would be resisted by all means at its disposal. But even if such movements were successfully contained, they would constitute a continuing source of internal stress and a disruptive factor in Israel's relations with the Palestinian state, and perhaps with other Arab states as well. The potential impact of a Palestinian state on the political behavior of Israeli Arabs is therefore of utmost concern to Israel.

In most respects, Israeli Arabs appear to have accommodated themselves to the reality of their status as a minority in a Jewish state. While it would be an exaggeration to see in their behavior ideological legitimation of this situation, it is true, nonetheless, that Israeli Arabs have generally acted as if they recognized the irreversibility of the decision of history in 1948.

Thus, Israeli Arab politics usually take place within the institutional parameters of the state, security offenses have been relatively infrequent, and violent expressions of collective discontent (for example, Land Day demonstrations in 1976) have been so exceptional that they are newsworthy events. Participation in the Israeli electoral system has been high (with the majority of Arab votes in every election being cast for Zionist or Zionist-affiliated lists), and significant numbers of Arabs are not just reconciled to the need for moderation, but actively promote Jewish-Arab coexistence and cooperation.

At the same time, there is considerable evidence of political radicalization since 1967, and especially since 1973, manifested in increasing self-identification as Palestinians and alienation from Israeli political norms and institutions.[3] This phenomenon is generally attributed to two factors—the encounter with the Palestinians of the West Bank and Gaza, reinforced by the enhanced prestige of the PLO after 1973, and the growing sense of relative socioeconomic deprivation (with Israeli Jews as the designated reference group), particularly among the Arab intelligentsia, for whom expectations of professional satisfaction commensurate with self-perceived status are most likely to be frustrated.[4]

Whether an independent Palestinian state would intensify this process of alienation is a matter of dispute. Some have argued that a resolution of the Israeli-Palestinian conflict would eliminate the tension currently felt by Israeli Arabs between their cultural affinity and their political identity, and that in the aftermath of a settlement, they could more easily concentrate on their social-civic concerns within Israel and even serve as an economic and cultural force for peace between the two states.[5] Activists in Rakah (the New Communist List, which enjoys widespread support, especially among younger Arabs) have been particularly forceful in their assertions that the pre-1967 borders represent final peace borders and that after peace, Arabs living within these borders would simply be a national minority, like the Hungarian minority in Rumania, entitled to ambiguously defined "civil and national rights" but to whom the right of self-determination would not apply.[6]

Others are convinced that a Palestinian state would merely sharpen the duality of Israeli Arab loyalties and further stimulate secessionist tendencies.[7] This conviction is grounded in a number of potential effects of Palestinian independence in the West Bank and Gaza. The mere existence of a Palestinian state in such close proximity is liable to provide emotional sustenance to those Israeli Arab circles who already define themselves exclusively as an integral part of the Palestinian people. A 1975 survey that dichotomized Palestinian and Israeli self-identity revealed that 41 percent of Israeli Arabs claimed the former while only 29 percent chose the latter, and this gap has almost certainly grown in subsequent years.[8] The political inclinations of the first group are expressed in organizations such as *Abna al-Balad* ("sons of the village" or "sons of the homeland") and its student faction, the Progressive National Movement, which condemn Rakah for its moderation and endorse the leadership of the PLO. Their position on the question of the proper disposition of the Arab-populated areas of Israel may be inferred from a 1977 Manifesto of the Arab Students Committee (the Hebrew University branch of the PNM), which called for self-determination for "the masses of the Galilee and the Triangle."[9] The extent to which such "Palestinization" has taken hold among Israeli Arabs is difficult to determine, but one informed observer suggests that Rakah finds the greatest challenge to its preeminence precisely from this direction, rather than from more Israel-oriented Arab forces.[10]

A Palestinian state may further stimulate these tendencies through an assertive cultural nationalism which, because of close proximity, will be simultaneously transmitted (through radio and television broadcasts, newspapers, personal contact) to Israeli Arabs. But even if the Palestinian state's overt message is restrained, its day-to-day functioning may intensify the alienation of Israeli Arabs, particularly of the most politically ambitious, active, and upwardly mobile among them. For independence will provide avenues of personal advancement for residents of the Palestinian state—in politics, bureaucracy, diplomacy, the military, the judiciary, and in quasi-public economic and social institutions—which will remain limited for

Arabs in Israel as long as Israel retains its essentially Jewish vocation. The frustration engendered by the "demonstration effect" may be somewhat mitigated by actual emigration to the Palestinian state of the most alienated Arabs, and one study does demonstrate a high correlation between Palestinian self-identity and willingness to move to the new state.[11] But the ideological-national attractiveness of the Palestinian state may well exceed its physical attractiveness — which will depend more on its concrete character, political regime, religious coloration, economic system and performance, and so on. Regardless of the extent of emigration, large numbers of Arabs will remain within the postsettlement borders of Israel, some of them inclined to attempt to alter those borders. Furthermore, indigenous secessionist movements may be supported by the Palestinian state and/or other Arab states, if not with funds or weapons, then at least through a political and propaganda campaign appropriate to a continuation of the Palestinian struggle by other means.

It is most unlikely that Israel could successfully compete with a Palestinian state for the emotional loyalties of Israeli Arabs. A more realistic guiding principle for Israel's "domestic Arab policy" would be to strive for a situation in which the political behavior of Israeli Arabs did not threaten the continuing territorial integrity of the state. Such a situation might result from a series of measures designed to minimize the incentives to and potential effectiveness of secessionist activities and maximize the disincentives of such activities.

The receptivity of Israeli Arabs to secessionist appeals is only in part a function of abstract ideological preferences. It is also related to the degree to which their economic and social expectations are satisfied. One way to reduce the level of frustration, especially among the intelligentsia, is to lower expectations by providing better academic and career guidance. A disproportionate number of Arab students choose the literary stream in secondary school and the humanities or "soft" social sciences in university, often with an emphasis on Arab studies (language, literature, religion), which best prepares them for financially unrewarding and progressively less prestigious teaching posts.[12] Acquisition of skills more appropriate to opportunities offered in the general economy (vocational, technical, engineering) could reduce the distance between expectations raised by academic education and the actual rewards. A related measure would be a concentrated effort to remove bureaucratic obstacles (zoning or licensing bottlenecks) to residential construction, since the housing shortage in the Arab sector is often a cause of generalized resentment of the authorities.

Simultaneously, steps could be taken to undermine the rationale of secessionism by diminishing the size and contiguity of areas characterized as Arab. In practice, this would mean dispersing the Jewish population, especially in Western and Central Galilee, by all means short of widespread expropriation of privately owned Arab land. With continued Jewish settlement in the West Bank and Gaza almost certainly precluded by the creation of a Palestinian state there, resources and manpower would become available for this purpose. The demographic base for potential secessionist movements might also be curtailed by some administrative actions and territorial aspects of the peace settlement. Administratively, all residents of Israel could, on the basis of a declaration of loyalty, be required to choose between Israeli or Palestinian citizenship. Those who chose the latter, perhaps for emotional reasons, could retain the status of permanent residents in Israel and be protected by its laws, but they would be denied certain political privileges (the right to vote, the right to run for office, for example). This measure might be supplemented by territorial arrangements that could have the effect of transferring several tens of thousands of Israeli Arabs to the Palestinian state.

Finally, security and judicial disincentives to secessionist activity should be swift and unequivocal. Secessionism in general would be illegal. If the definition of impermissible activities is clearly communicated and the consequences of violations — including deportation of noncitizens — properly specified, a substantial proportion of those who remain alienated despite other, more positive, measures may nevertheless be deterred from translating their inclinations into action, and induced to exercise the option of "exit" rather than "voice."

All these programs, however, cannot alter fundamental cultural-historical facts and will not completely eliminate the problem of irredenta. Whatever residual threat remains must therefore be viewed as a risk of a Palestinian state. What is less clear is whether that risk is more or less dangerous than the future character of Jewish-Arab relations in Israel in the absence of a peace settlement or as a result of some other kind of settlement. On this issue, only some tentative speculation is possible. In the absence of any peace, internal tensions in Israel are likely to continue to grow anyway, a joint function of national conflict and social discontent fueled by low Arab access to resources not allocated to defense. It is even possible, though not probable, that at some point, the situation may be more explosive than that engendered by a Palestinian state. A Jordanian regime in the West Bank and, perhaps, Gaza would probably be less attractive emotionally to Israeli Arabs, and it might mitigate the problem of divided loyalties, but it would not eliminate resentment caused by cultural alienation or relative opportunity deprivation.

On balance, then, the effect of a Palestinian state on Israeli Arabs is liable to be more detrimental from Israel's perspective than a continuation of the status quo — but not to the point where this consideration outweighs the other advantages of a settlement. It might also be more destabilizing than a Jordanian settlement — but not to a degree sufficient to compensate for the other defects of a non-Palestinian settlement. Whatever course is adopted, serious problems will remain, but the marginal impact of a Palestinian state, if properly anticipated, is not so great that it should constitute a decisive factor in Israeli policy.

The status of Israeli settlements

As of March 1981, there were eighty-five settlements built or under construction in the West Bank, with a combined population of about 18,500.[13] According to government claims, this contrasted with a total of twenty-four settlements, housing about 3,200 inhabitants, when the Likud took office in May 1977.[14] Estimates of the land area of these settlements range from 110,500 dunams[15] to 200,000 dunams,[16] that is, 2–3.6 percent of the total area of the West Bank, or 6.9–12.4 percent of the area under cultivation. Some of the settlements are little more than paramilitary outposts—a few trailers on blocks surrounded by wire fence—intended to demonstrate "presence," but others are very substantial agricultural or residential undertakings, often with profound Jewish historical connotations. A Palestinian state would certainly prevent further settlement, and might possibly mean the dissolution of those existing now.

Although there is fairly widespread consensus within Israel on the intrinsic right of Jews to settle in Judaea and Samaria, differences exist over the advisability of exercising that right and the extent to which these settlements serve Israel's military-security interests, as opposed to its ideological aspirations. Until 1977, Labor-dominated governments tended to emphasize the trip-wire and antiterrorist functions of settlements and concentrated the settlement effort in the Jordan Valley, to which Labor security doctrine ascribed paramount importance. Even within this framework, the immediate security value of civilian settlements (as opposed to military outposts) was a subject of dispute, and settlement policy was arguably as much a product of the government's ultimate territorial aspirations—unofficially embodied in the Allon Plan—as of current security needs. But whatever the motivations, fourteen of the twenty-four West Bank settlements established before May 1977 were located in the sparsely populated Jordan Valley.[17] The other ten, including five in the Etzion Bloc southwest of Bethlehem, were almost all the result of private pressure and initiative and ex post facto government approval.

The guiding principles of the Likud government were rather different. Religious-historical claims played a much more prominent role in the Likud approach to Judaea and Samaria. Furthermore, there was a conviction, articulated by then-Agriculture Minister Ariel Sharon, that "*every* settlement has its purpose and role in the defense of Israel," and, more generally, that control of the area could not be ensured without a major change in the demographic balance.[18] The Likud therefore proposed to settle extensively the whole of Judaea and Samaria, including the densely populated uplands. Underlying this approach was the intention to create a permanent Jewish presence throughout the territories of such proportions as to exclude the possibility of their subsequent transmission to another sovereignty. Thus, most of the settlements established since 1977 have been located along the mountain ridge or in the western foothills, and in many cases, immediate security considerations were clearly of secondary importance. In 1979, for example, the High Court of Justice disallowed the allocation of private land belonging to villagers of Rujayb, near Nablus, to the settlement of Eilon Moreh, because it was convinced that the security arguments used by the government to justify the land seizure were marginal, if not altogether specious.[19]

If the purpose of the government has been to create irreversible physical and political facts, the results have been mixed. On the one hand, the effect on the demographic balance has been negligible. Despite a massive investment in settlement infrastructure, the total number of Jews living in the West Bank is hardly greater than the natural increase in the Arab population for 1980 alone. On the other hand, the large number of settlements and their physical dispersion have converted the West Bank into a crazy quilt of intermingled Jewish and Arab areas which, if subject to separate sovereign authority, would produce a political, administrative, and economic situation of nightmarish and probably untenable complexity.

This prospect, as much as the unlikelihood of securing Palestinian agreement to extraterritorial status for these settlements and the force of the precedent established in Sinai, requires Israel to weigh the benefits and costs of maintaining the settlements should they become an obstacle to an otherwise-attainable peace agreement.

In the present circumstances, the foremost benefit of the settlements is the reinforcement of Israel's ultimate claim to the West Bank, primarily by reducing the ability of any Israeli government — for domestic political reasons — to renounce that claim. Militarily, the value of the settlements is mixed, at best. Although they are allotted a role in area defense — many settlements have passive defenses (mines, wire) and also maintain substantial stocks of infantry and antitank weapons – their ability to withstand an assault by modern armored and mechanized forces (unlike those which Jewish settlements faced in 1948) is certainly inferior to that of regular army formations. In the event of a surprise attack, fortified settlements might conceivably delay enemy advances until army forces arrived to assume the defense, but it is just as likely, if not more so, that the evacuation of exposed settlements would demand first priority (as happened in the Golan Heights in 1973), causing traffic congestion and the diversion of combat units from other missions. Settlements are sometimes said to contribute to the antiterrorism campaign, but the settlers themselves also constitute targets of attack; in the most bloody incident to date, six residents of Kiryat Arba, near Hebron, were ambushed and killed in the spring of 1980. The settlements' ability to contribute to Israeli defense and even to provide for their own security depends, at the very least, on the existence of an administration that allows them to be fortified and armed while enforcing the disarmament of the Arab population. Indeed, it has been argued that their ultimate survival requires the continuing protection of the Israeli army.[20] These circumstances would not obtain in an independent Palestinian state. In their absence, Jewish settlements, even with extraterritorial status, might be transformed into vulnerable outposts of little strategic value – at best, hostages to Palestinian demands on other issues; at worst, victims of rejectionist efforts to destroy them, incorporate them, or harass them in order to erode the whole fabric of peace.

Economically, too, the settlements appear to represent more of a liability than an asset. Despite the massive sums already invested in them, most of them continue to require infusions of treasury funds. According to one calculation, visible expenditure on settlements in 1980 alone amounted to about $265 million, or more than 6 percent of the budget for nondefense, non-debt service items, and government economists estimated that $1 billion was spent on West Bank settlement between 1977 and 1981.[21] These were funds diverted from other purposes, whether social investment or settlement of the Upper Galilee, which was relatively neglected after 1967, during a pe-

riod when the Arab demographic preponderance there continued to grow.[22] It may be argued, of course, that this money is
already spent, and that evacuating the West Bank settlements
would not bring it back. Part of the investment in settlements,
however, could be recovered. Some of the facilities (machinery,
equipment, and modular housing, for example) could be
relocated to Israel; some assets could either be sold to the new
Palestinian government (fixed housing) or retained under Israeli
ownership (industrial plant for joint economic enterprises). The
land and water (15 million cubic meters per year[23]) made available for the new state would enhance its ability to liquidate the
refugee problem and absorb others — including Israeli Arabs —
interested in moving there. In this latter eventuality, the economic cost would be offset, at least partially, by a process
clearly serving Israel's political interests.

All these considerations suggest that the maintenance of the
present settlement network, under Palestinian jurisdiction or
even on an extraterritorial basis, might not be desirable in practice, even if it were diplomatically attainable. Nevertheless, the
disestablishment of Jewish settlements would entail very high
costs — political as well as economic. Indeed, the most ominous
cost would probably be domestic strife in Israel itself. Many of
the settlers in the West Bank are motivated by very deep ideological or religious commitments. These people are far less likely
than were settlers in Sinai to view material compensation as
relevant in any degree, and it is certain that they would actively
resist evacuation, perhaps to the point of armed confrontation.
Furthermore, their activities benefit from widespread sympathy
throughout Israeli society.[24] Not only is the emotional attachment to Judaea and Samaria great; the bitterness engendered by
the Sinai withdrawal itself makes Israeli acceptance of another
arrangement involving the forcible evacuation of settlers virtually inconceivable. For despite the usual tendency of public
opinion to follow government leadership on foreign affairs and
defense matters, a government concession on this issue, with all
its emotional saliency, would still provoke militant resistance,
backed by broad public support and on a scale far exceeding
that witnessed in Sinai.

But if the specter of domestic upheaval is sufficient to deter any Israeli government, not just from uprooting settlements, but even from acquiescing in their transfer to non-Israeli jurisdiction, then one rationale of the settlement effort — whether implicit and restrained before 1977 or explicit and unrestrained since then — would be proved correct. On the other hand, civil strife on this issue cannot be altogether avoided except by a status for the settlements that either precludes peace, and thus entails the costs and risks of the status quo, or else produces, in the case of extraterritoriality, a peace whose value is minimized by its inherent fragility. Resolving this contradiction and mitigating the danger of civil conflict in Israel might be possible if a peace agreement provides for an alternative to both the Sinai precedent and the incorporation of the settlements into Israel.

Although the smallest of the outposts might be dismantled without undue disruption, the only workable arrangement for most of the established settlements may therefore well be one that offers settlers who do not come under Israeli sovereignty — as a result of territorial adjustments — a choice between relocation with compensation or residence in the Palestinian state under conditions similar to those of Arabs living in Israel.

The status of Jerusalem

Unlike security, economic, or other territorial issues, the issue of Jerusalem is of such intense emotional centrality that it virtually defies a rational cost-benefit calculus. For Jews, Jerusalem is the wellspring of their collective identity. As the ancient capital of Judaea and the only city with an uninterrupted Jewish presence since the dispersion, it has been the focus of hopes and prayers throughout Jewish history. In the modern era, the renewal of Jewish settlement in Palestine concentrated on Jerusalem, which has had a Jewish majority since the second quarter of the nineteenth century.[25] The first secular vision of redemption, inspired by the political revival of Italy, was elaborated by Moses Hess in a volume entitled *Rome and Jeru-*

salem. And the emerging Jewish national movement was called, almost inevitably, after Jerusalem's biblical name — Zion.

It was therefore natural that Jerusalem be declared the capital of the newly independent State of Israel. But the euphoria of national revival was marred by the partition of the city in 1948. For the next nineteen years, Jews were physically alienated from East Jerusalem, including the Old City, which represented the most tangible thread in the historical memory that fired the passion for Jewish national rebirth. Thus, when Jerusalem was reunited in 1967 (Map IX), it was as if a continuing trauma had suddenly dissipated; the liberation of the city was viewed by many — and not just the religious — as a prophetic fulfillment, an event of cosmic and quasi-mystical proportions.

The historical attachment to Jerusalem is reinforced by the living memory of Jewish blood shed for its sake. In the 1948 War of Independence, fully one-third of Jewish casualties were incurred in bitter battles in or for Jerusalem (including Latrun), and the struggle for Jerusalem in 1967 made it the costliest single engagement of the Six-Day War. Jerusalem has therefore become a transcendental value for Israelis, not an instrument to promote some larger end but an intrinsic part of the collective purpose itself, and if there is any outstanding issue about which it can truly be said that an Israeli national consensus exists, it is that Jerusalem remain the capital of Israel, undivided and wholly accessible.[26]

The annexation of East Jerusalem on June 28, 1967, highlighted the unique significance to Israel of the city, and every measure taken since then has been intended to underscore the irreversibility of this act. Thus, the complete administrative integration of the city was followed by extensive economic integration. The Jewish Quarter in the heart of the Old City was reconstructed, and large Jewish housing estates were built to the north, east, and south of Arab-populated East Jerusalem in order to make manifest the city's detachment from the rest of the West Bank and its incorporation into Israel.

Yet despite all these measures, East Jerusalem remains in many respects the heart of the West Bank. With over 110,000 Arab residents, it is the largest Arab urban center in the area.[27]

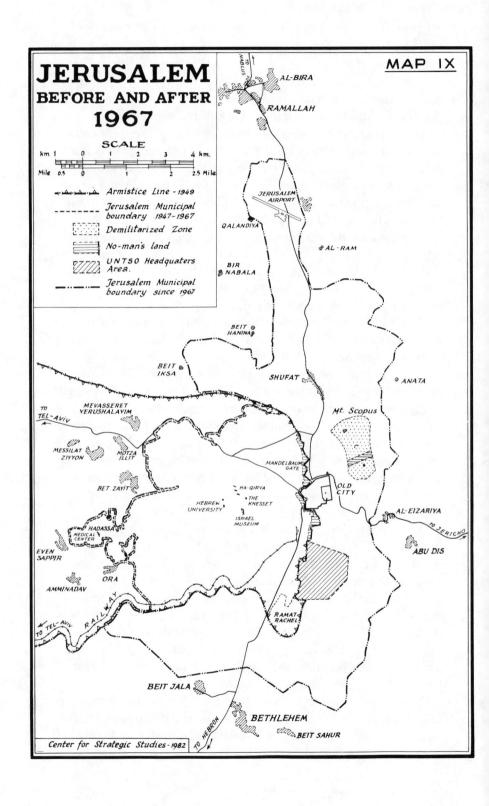

JERUSALEM
BEFORE AND AFTER
1967

MAP IX

SCALE

km. 1   0   1   2   3   4 km.

Mile 0.5   0   1   2   2.5 Mile

.–.–.–. Armistice Line - 1949

- - - - Jerusalem Municipal
          boundary 1947-1967

          Demilitarized Zone

          No-man's land

          UNTSO Headquaters
          Area.

          Jerusalem Municipal
          boundary since 1967

TO NABLUS

AL-BIRA

RAMALLAH

JERUSALEM AIRPORT

QALANDIYA

AL-RAM

BIR NABALA

BEIT HANINA

BEIT IKSA

SHUFAT

ANATA

TO TEL-AVIV

MEVASSERET YERUSHALAYIM

Mt. Scopus

MESSILAT ZIYYON

MOTZA ILLIT

MANDELBAUM GATE

BET ZAYIT

HA-QIRYA

OLD CITY

HEBREW UNIVERSITY

THE KNESSET

ISRAEL MUSEUM

AL-EIZARIYA

TO JERICHO

HADASSA MEDICAL CENTER

ABU DIS

EVEN SAPPIR

ORA

AMMINADAV

RAILWAY

RAMAT RACHEL

TO TEL-AVIV

BEIT JALA

BETHLEHEM

TO HEBRON

BEIT SAHUR

Center for Strategic Studies - 1982

Geographically, it straddles the Nablus-Hebron road and links the two main subregions of the West Bank. It houses many of the West Bank's most important social and quasi-political institutions, such as the Supreme Muslim Council, the West Bank Labor Federation, the Federation of Charitable Societies, the Organization of West Bank Chambers of Commerce, and the Association of Arab Free Professionals. The three daily newspapers that serve the occupied territories — al-Quds (Jerusalem), al-Sh'ab (The People), and al-Fajr (The Dawn) — are all published here. And its inhabitants include the largest concentration of administrators, professionals, journalists, religious dignitaries, businessmen, and — perhaps most important — prominent political figures.

In addition, Jerusalem plays a role in Palestinian Arab conciousness somewhat analogous, if not identical, to its role in Jewish cultural-national sentiment. There is no historical precedent for Palestinian independence on which to draw, so the explicitly political connotations of Jerusalem are muted. Indeed, even in the broader Arab context, Jerusalem was never given political pride of place, having been subordinated to other capitals during the periods of Arab rule in Palestine. However, the city's cultural and religious preeminence arouses emotional associations strong enough to make a voluntary abdication of all political claims to Jerusalem inconceivable, not just for Palestinians, but for the whole of their Arab-Islamic hinterland. Jerusalem is the site of the holiest Muslim shrines on Palestinian soil, some of them intimately connected with the life of Muhammad. Within its precincts, argues a noted Palestinian historian, "are buried countless generations of Muslim saints and scholars, warriors and leaders. It evokes the proudest Palestinian and Arab historical memories . . . It is the natural capital of Arab Palestine."[28]

It is fairly evident that Israeli and Palestinian aspirations concerning Jerusalem cannot be reconciled by any conventional political formula. Because sovereignty is indivisible, Israeli and Palestinian claims in their present incarnations are mutually exclusive. The incompatibility of the respective positions is exacerbated, perhaps ironically, by the fact that the major contradictions are more symbolic than practical. This is so because the existence of a political boundary between East Jerusalem and the rest of the West Bank would not necessarily prevent intense and intimate ties between the two entities or the full expression of Arab cultural and religious interests within the city.

Even under the current regime, in which East Jerusalem is formally part of the State of Israel, the links between Jerusalem and the West Bank persist. In addition to the organizational connection already documented, the two entities have a common upper-school curriculum (though subject to different administrative jurisdictions), and East Jerusalemites, while required to bear Israeli identity cards, retain a citizenship (currently Jordanian) in common with West Bankers. Inside the city, Islamic and Christian institutions — mosques, churches, schools, shrines, cemeteries, health and welfare facilities, *waqf* (Islamic charitable endowment) properties — are administered independently by the appropriate religious bodies. In short, many of the Palestinian associations with Jerusalem are realized now, and could be preserved by a formalization of the status quo even if no part of Jerusalem belonged juridically to the Palestinian state.

Exclusive Israeli sovereignty does, however, negate the symbolic and political components of the Palestinian demand for jurisdiction, and any proposal for Jerusalem which incorporates the basic Israeli position, no matter how creative in terms of municipal structure or otherwise devolutionary in terms of communal autonomy, founders on this basic obstacle.[29] But any proposals which radically differ from this position threaten Israeli values at least as profound as any Palestinian urge for self-determination. A mutually acceptable solution is therefore possible, if at all, only if the question of sovereignty is deliberately obfuscated to the point where all parties can credibly claim that they have secured their essential objectives. Such an approach is difficult, perhaps unprecedented, and likely to result in an inelegant and organizationally cumbersome entity, but the complexity of the issue and the depth of emotions almost certainly render a more conventional approach self-defeating.

In the case of Israel, essential objectives would appear to be the following:

(1) the physical and administrative unity of the city;

(2) free and secure access to any part of the city and control of those sites of peculiar religious, historical, or cultural value to Jews;

(3) its retention as a strategic bulwark on top of the central mountain ridge;

(4) the legitimation of its status as Israel's capital.

These objectives can be achieved by a peace settlement that leaves Jerusalem intact as a single municipal entity. Physical division of the city is impossible, not only for obvious political reasons, but also for the very practical reason that an intermingling of population has already taken place on a scale far exceeding that in the rest of the West Bank.[30] Furthermore, physical unity per se may not be a major political obstacle, since many Palestinians who address the Jerusalem issue in its national context also recognize the inevitability and desirability of an open, united city.[31]

The unity of the city does not necessarily require a perpetuation of the current regime, however. It can also be preserved by a distribution of power according to functional needs, one that could also accommodate some Palestinian aspirations without negating Israeli interests in the city. While a detailed and technically competent treatment of the issue would clearly be necessary at some point in the negotiations, it is possible to foresee the kind of administrative structure that would conform, in general, to these guiding principles.

The basis of the formula would be a provision allowing residents of Jerusalem to opt for either Israeli or Palestinian citizenship and to participate simultaneously in the national politics of their state and in the administration of the city. Jerusalem itself could be governed by a Jewish mayor and a Palestinian deputy-mayor, elected in a city-wide ballot, and a municipal council consisting of neighborhood or district representatives chosen through personal and direct elections.

The municipal government would bear city-wide responsibility for those services which are least culture-specific and most appropriate for large-scale government structures (for example, fire fighting, urban transportation, water and sewage, electricity, sanitation, road building, and land zoning). It would also assume some of the functions currently borne by the central government (for example, vehicle licensing, postal services), both to desensitize the issue of sovereignty symbols and to provide a source of municipal revenue. Finally, the municipal administration would oversee a separate Jerusalem police force, formally subordinate to neither the Israeli nor Palestinian governments, whose main purpose would be to ensure internal security and freedom of movement and access within the city. This would be a mixed force (as is the present Jerusalem district police), but its high command, along with the command of its most critical branches (intelligence, special operations, and so on) would be in the hands of officers seconded from the Israel Police. Any immigration, customs, or security procedures applying to movement between the two states could be implemented at the northern, eastern, southern, and western exits of the city by the appropriate national authorities, thus ensuring free movement into and within Jerusalem itself. The activities of the municipal government could be financed by property and sales taxes and license fees. Income taxes could be collected either by the municipal government itself, on the basis of unified rates, or by the central government of the states of which Jerusalem residents had declared themselves citizens. In the latter case, a special provision would be necessary for those who are not citizens of either state.

Although the municipal government itself would be fully bilingual, services more subject to cultural-identity sensitivities, especially public education, could fall within the purview of lower-level structures — boroughs or neighborhood councils — corresponding to religioethnic residence patterns. Private educational facilities, of course, would continue to operate, but the character of public education — curriculum and language of instruction — would be determined by the character of the different neighborhoods. In fact, neighborhood councils would be needed primarily to provide auxiliary support services, since curriculum, staffing, supervision, and certification could, for all practical purposes, be assigned to the education departments of the respective national authorities, which could also finance these aspects of Jerusalem education. The main support services — school building and maintenance — along with local parks and recreation programs, cultural activities, libraries, and such, could then be supervised by the borough or neighborhood councils and paid for by some combination of local contributions, municipal grants-in-aid (on a per capita or per capita income tax basis), and support from the religiocultural hinterlands of the Jewish, Christian, and Muslim communities of Jerusalem.

As a result of the existence of boroughs or neighborhoods, Jerusalem would be crisscrossed by local jurisdictional limits that would permit community-specific solidarity events (celebration of holidays, display of symbols) without impairing the day-to-day functioning of the city as a unified organism. Some of these limits might coincide with a line running from Ophel Street through Dung Gate, along the Western Wall and around the Jewish Quarter, up the Street of the Armenians to Jaffa Gate, along the Old City Wall to a point just west of Damascus Gate, and then northward, parallel to the Nablus Road, in the direction of Sheikh Jarrah (Map X). These limits would have no more practical implications for sovereignty than any others, but they might provide a reference point sufficiently ambiguous to be both ignored by Israeli cartographers and noticed by Palestinian ones. The only real change in the city's present geographical configuration might therefore be the transmission to Palestinian sovereignty of the Qalandiya "finger" north of the Neve Ya'aqov road. This would provide the Palestinian state with a functioning airport (on the clear understanding that no other airfields — civilian or military — would be operated or built by that state); it would also reduce the Arab population weight within the city, thus alleviating Israeli concerns that demographic changes might later destabilize the municipal status quo.

POSSIBLE NEIGHBOURHOOD COUNCIL AREAS
IN A UNITED JERUSALEM

SCALE

km. 1   0   1   2   3   4 km.
Mile 0.5 0   1   2   2.5 Mile

Jewish Neighbourhood

Arab Neighbourhood

Area to be transferred to a Palestinian State.

MAP X

AL-BIRA

DIR DIBWAN

RAMALLAH

BEITUNIYA

QALANDIYA

AL-RAM

AL-JIB

BIR NABALA

NEVE YA'AQOV

AL NABI SAMWIL

BIDDU

BEIT HANINA

GIVAT ZEEV

BEIT SURIK

BEIT IKSA

RAMOT

SHUFAT

ANATA

MEVASSERET YERUSHALAYIM

RAMOT ESHKOL

GIVAT SHAPIRA

TEL-AVIV

SANHEDRIYYA

ISAWIYA

MESSILAT ZIYYON

MOTZA ILLIT

MOTZA

GIVAT SHAUL

ROMEMA

MEQOR BARUKH

SHEIKH JARRAH

KEFAR SHAUL

QIRYAT MOSHE

MEA SHEARIM

WADI AL-JOZ

BET ZAYIT

BET HA-KEREM

HAQIRYA

OLD CITY

AL-TUR

QIRYAT HA-UNIVERSITA

REHAVYA

TO JERICHO

EVEN SAPPIR

QIRYAT HADASSA

EIN KEREM

BAYIT VE-GAN

NEVE SHAANAN

YEMIN MOSHE

QIRYAT SHMUEL

JEWISH QUARTER

SILWAN

AL-EIZARIYA

EMEQ REFAIM

ORA

GIVAT MORDEKHAY

ABU-DIS

AMMINADAV

QIRYAT HA-YOVEL

GONEN

MANAHAT

MEQOR HAYYIM

TALPIYYOT

TALPIYYOT EAST

ARAB AL-SAWAHIRA

TEL-AVIV

RAILWAY

SHARAFAT

BEIT SAFAFA

RAMAT RAHEL

SUR-BAHIR

BATTIR

GILLO

BEIT JALA

BETHLEHEM

BEIT SAHUR

HEBRON

Center for Strategic Studies - 1982

Insofar as the properties, holy places, and special interests of the different religions are concerned, these should also be removed from the formal jurisdiction of any national authority and placed under the supervision of the municipal government, with the clear intention of retaining the present system of self-administration by the different religions. In practice, the closest possible coordination could be maintained — perhaps on the basis of nomination — between the Chief Rabbinate of Israel and the Chief Rabbinate of Jerusalem, with the Muslim and various Christian institutions relying on whatever informal personnel arrangements were most convenient to them. In this way, the protection of Jewish religious sites and interests in Jerusalem could be maintained without the explicit involvement of any sovereign national government.

Only on the question of military deployments in the Jerusalem region would there be any departure from the principle of apparent equality. If Israeli forces were withdrawn from the rest of the West Bank, Jerusalem would constitute the only remaining Israeli military foothold on top of the central mountain ridge. Maintaining this foothold would be essential, either as an established base area from which to proceed to engage as far east as possible an impending invasion from across the Jordan River, or, in the very worst case, as a large and topographically favorable defensive bulwark controlling one of the major axes of advance into the coastal plain itself. Retaining Jerusalem as a strategic bulwark might not require the stationing of forces inside the city itself, except perhaps for electronic observation posts on its eastern edge. But the emplacement of Israeli bases, equipment, stores, and other facilities up to the western municipal boundary would be a necessary exception to the general provision that the whole region, within a ten-kilometer radius of the Temple Mount, be completely demilitarized.

If an overall agreement incorporating these principles and provisions could be achieved, there is no reason why Jerusalem could not then serve as the capital of a Palestinian state, as well as of Israel. The location within the city of Palestinian government institutions (executive and legislative offices, Supreme Court, *Shari'a* Court of Appeal) and symbols of independence (foreign legations) would not detract from the essential unity of the city or from its stature as Israel's capital. Indeed, a mutually acceptable regulation of this sort, symbolized by the location in Jerusalem of Arab embassies to Israel, would end the legal ambiguity of the corpus separatum status assigned to Jerusalem in the 1947 UN partition scheme and permit other states to locate their embassies to Israel in Jerusalem as well. Thus, the international legitimation of Israel's claim to Jerusalem, though not unconditional, would finally be achieved.

Without provisions to safeguard its essential objectives in Jerusalem, Israel will undoubtedly reject any political settlement, and the threat of a Palestinian state to these objectives is really moot. Even the guidelines suggested here, though they do promise to preserve all of Israel's essential rights and interests in the city, probably represent the very limit of Israeli flexibility.

There is no assurance that an agreement of this sort can be secured; or, if attainable, that it would guarantee the city a future free of all tension and discontent. It is virtually certain, however, that exclusive Israeli sovereignty over the whole of Jerusalem will not be a mutually acceptable basis for peace, and the only apparent alternatives are a repartition of the city, which is abhorrent to almost all Israelis, or some sort of international regime in which Israel's status even in West Jerusalem would be undermined. If a Palestine-state (or any other) settlement implies some symbolic diminution of unilateral Israeli control of Jerusalem, that would not appear to be an intolerable cost to bear.

Economic implications for Israel

Just as the economic prospects of a Palestinian state are not as forbidding as is often supposed, so, too, do the negative economic implications for Israel of Palestinian independence appear to be frequently exaggerated. Even in the worst (and highly improbable) case, in which West Bank/Gaza markets, manpower, and resources were completely and suddenly closed to Israel, the overall damage to Israel's economy would be quickly reparable — except for the loss of water.

As a result of growing economic integration since 1967, the West Bank and Gaza have emerged as important markets for Israeli goods. By 1980, Israeli "exports" to the West Bank and Gaza amounted to I.S.3032.4 million of industrial and agricultural products, while "imports" were only I.S.1162.9 million.[32] The difference, which is registered for accounting purposes as a $344.7 million surplus in the merchandise category of Israel's foreign trade statistics, appears to be significant, especially in view of Israel's overall merchandise deficit of $3,379 million.[33] From an economic point of view, however, this trade is really internal. Since it is carried out in Israeli currency, its effect on Israel's foreign trade balance is negligible, and the argument that restricted Israeli access to West Bank/Gaza markets would cause a further deterioration in Israel's balance of payments is therefore misplaced.

Even as a "domestic" market, the territories fail to live up to their theoretical potential. The population of the West Bank/Gaza was approximately 30 percent of Israel's in 1980, but because of lower per capita income levels, the total purchasing power of the territories was only 7.5 percent of Israel's.[34] Furthermore, the sectors of the Israeli economy that have the greatest potential for dynamic future growth (science-based industry, aviation, electronics, off-season agriculture, and general research and development) are precisely those likely to find the West Bank/Gaza markets unpromising under any circumstances.

It is true that less sophisticated industries — agricultural products and processed foods, textiles and clothing, housewares and appliances — benefit from the accessibility of the West Bank/Gaza, because a larger market permits greater production efficiency (economies of scale) and higher profitability. In these industries, Israeli producers would probably feel some loss from administrative exclusion or competition with Palestinian producers operating under preferential conditions.

Furthermore, the elimination of the de facto customs union between Israel and the territories might have an unsavory noneconomic side effect. On goods currently imported into Israel (and the territories), Israel applies extremely high duties. If, as seems likely, a Palestinian state lowered the duties on these items, there would be a great temptation for criminal elements in Israel and the Palestinian state to join hands and organize the smuggling of such goods across the Israeli border.[35]

Nevertheless, it is quite possible that these potential costs would be compensated by new opportunities. A Palestinian state committed to national economic development would confront a wide range of planning problems, some of which might require the involvement of foreign consultants or contractors. In some fields — land reclamation, water planning, energy production (especially solar) and conservation, rural development, even immigrant absorption — Israel's proximity, its familiarity with the area, and its own analogous circumstances and experiences would leave it well placed to compete for such projects, at least on a commercial basis. Furthermore, a regional peace might open up much more significant markets in other Arab countries, hitherto closed to Israeli exporters. It is even possible that some Arab states might come to view a healthy Israeli economy as vital to Palestinian, and regional, stability.

Political sensitivities, of course, could work to Israel's disadvantage and Israeli opportunities might therefore be limited, especially in the first few years. But even if none of these potential opportunities ever materialized, the worst (and least likely) outcome would be a total loss of West Bank/Gaza markets to Israeli producers, and since the imports of the territories represented less than 12 percent of Israel's agricultural and industrial output in 1980, and only 3 percent of its GNP,[36] that loss would not be an intolerable cost to the Israeli economy as a whole.

The same general conclusion applies to the question of manpower. Because of the different scale and character of the Israeli and West Bank/Gaza economies, the benefits of labor mobility have been asymmetrical, as would be the costs of its termination. For while West Bank/Gaza workers in Israel constitute almost 35 percent of the labor force of the territories, they make up less than 6 percent of the total Israeli civilian labor force.[37] Thus, the imbalance of interest in continuing labor mobility is so clearly on the Palestinian side that a unilateral Palestinian decision to stop it is quite unlikely. Indeed, the threat to halt the flow of workers would be a much more potent political lever in Israeli hands than in Palestinian hands.

It is true, however, that the concentration of West Bank/ Gaza workers in a few branches of the economy distorts this overall picture. By 1980, these workers — mostly unskilled and semiskilled — comprised over 30 percent of agricultural employees in Israel and about 35 percent of construction workers.[38] Their sudden withdrawal would undoubtedly create manpower shortages for some Israeli employers. Short-term production schedules, especially in the packing and canning industries, would be disrupted and profitability would be affected by the ensuing rise in wage levels (just as wage levels in the West Bank/ Gaza would be depressed). Still, the adverse consequences of a worst-case labor scenario might not be wholly unmitigated. Higher wages might attract some of those Israelis who now refuse to engage in certain types of labor, thereby reducing unemployment and welfare expenditures of the central government.[39] *Gastarbeiter* (foreign workers) could be brought from more distant labor-exporting countries — even Egypt — although the social problems could be considerable. And in some branches, such as construction, the result might even be a long overdue modernization of production techniques, delayed since 1967 by the availability of relatively low-priced manpower. In short, the abrupt withdrawal of West Bank/Gaza workers, however improbable, would cause short-term difficulties for Israel which, while certainly disruptive, would hardly be catastrophic. And in the longer term, after some inevitable problems of adjustment, the overall consequences might actually be beneficial.

Finally, there is a potential risk that Israeli access to West Bank/Gaza resources other than labor might be curtailed. Israeli dependence on raw materials from these areas is low, precisely because they are so poorly endowed. The one commodity for which a substantial Israeli demand has developed is building stone. When quarries in Judaea were struck in September of 1980, Israeli construction projects in the Jerusalem area fell behind schedule.[40] But aside from building stone, the only West Bank/Gaza resource upon which Israel is dependent is water.

Israel currently draws about 300 million cubic meters of

water per year — 18 percent of its total consumption — from the subterranean aquifer (the Yarkon-Taninim basin) that straddles the Israel-West Bank border.[41] It is possible for Israel to use this water without impinging on West Bank needs or overexploiting reserves and risking excessive salination, primarily because West Bank demands are now moderate — about 113–120 million cubic meters a year.[42] Of this total, approximately 100 million is used to water the 85,200 dunams of citrus and vegetables under irrigation. Much of the West Bank is not suitable for irrigation because of topography and soil conditions. Still an independent state committed to agricultural development would be able to locate at least 100,000 additional dunams worth irrigating, most of it west of the mountain ridge, requiring an increase of as much as 100 million cubic meters per year over current supply (based on current use rates). However, a capital-intensive program to install storage and distribution facilities for a sprinkler or drip system could eliminate most of the evaporation losses attributable to the open-ditch flood method that now characterizes much of West Bank farming, thus reducing the use rate by half and allowing the remaining supply to be diverted to new irrigation projects.[43] Theoretically at least, the area under irrigation could therefore be doubled without increasing the demand for water. However, long lead times and fragmented holdings mean that some additional pumping of groundwater — perhaps as much as 40–50 million cubic meters — would be inevitable.[44] Some of this might come from the eastern aquifer, which would not affect supplies to Israel, but much would be drawn from the western aquifer, which would reduce the amount available to Israel and raise the salinity of the remaining flow. The effect on Israeli agriculture, in general, would be detrimental, and many Israeli farms would have to be abandoned.

It is therefore necessary, from Israel's point of view, that an agreement be reached limiting Palestinian pumping of water west of the water divide. This agreement might include Israeli technological assistance (irrigation systems, hothouse techniques, and so forth) that would reduce the West Bank's need to draw on groundwater reserves, but since Israel's own water balance is so delicate and critical, some agreement to prevent overpumping of the western aquifer is indispensable. The fragmented nature of the Palestinian state would make such an agreement enforceable. For just as Israel would be vulnerable to West Bank overpumping, so would the Gaza Strip be vulnerable to Israeli overpumping. Gaza water is already growing brackish because of local overdrawing, and stepped-up Israeli pumping to the east of the Gaza Strip, to compensate for reduced flows in the Yarkon-Taninim basin, would adversely affect current agricultural production in Gaza and make further expansion there altogether impossible.

This leverage would disappear if Gaza received large quantities of water from the Nile (although that might make the Palestinian state uncomfortably dependent on Egyptian goodwill), in which case Israel would have to rely on other means to prevent the implementation of the potential threat to its water supplies implied by Palestinian independence. In the longer run, of course, the optimal solution to these problems would be a comprehensive regional water plan, including the introduction of large-scale desalination projects and the involvement of other states with water surpluses in regional sharing schemes. But until that became possible, a bilateral agreement covering the subterranean aquifer west of the mountain ridge would be indispensable.

6

Israeli Requirements for Risk Minimization

It is clear that a peace settlement based on the creation of an independent Palestinian state in the West Bank and Gaza entails certain risks and costs to Israeli security and other interests. The actual consequences of such a settlement are more a function of the probable dynamics of the environment after peace and the character of the Palestinian state than of the mere fact of its existence. To minimize the potential damage, a settlement must somehow effect a delicate balance between two types of elements: those that enhance Palestinian and Arab interest in its durability — that is, that strengthen their willingness and ability to abide by its provisions — and those that enhance Israel's ability to contain the consequences of possible breakdown — that is, that provide a margin of safety in the event that Arab revisionism, despite everything, should ultimately triumph.

A settlement that is too ambitious in terms of Israel's margin of safety may create such disappointment and bitterness among Palestinians that it will be an exposed and vulnerable target of subsequent destabilization efforts. A settlement that makes insufficient provision for the possibility of breakdown is not only imprudent but may also promote that very outcome by distorting the cost-benefit calculus of potential revisionists. The optimal balance between these two tendencies is inherently difficult to design, but the search for the best formula, in its various dimensions, should at least be guided by the major Israeli strategic objective — the minimization of the collective Arab threat to Israeli security. In practice, this would mean the inclusion in the settlement of political-diplomatic, military, spatial, and temporal elements intended to minimize the Palestinian and Arab incentive to challenge the peace, minimize their capacity to exploit the potential opportunities created by Israeli withdrawal, rationalize as much as possible the territorial arrangements, and insert a mechanism to evaluate the implementation of the settlement and build mutual confidence.

Political-diplomatic elements

The most effective means by which to minimize the Arab incentive to challenge the peace is to eliminate the Palestinian issue from Arab-Israeli relations. If this is achieved, regional politics thereafter might still be subject to the periodic tensions and conflicts that characterize normal international relations, but the fundamental ideological-theological contradiction that characterizes the current state of relations would have been removed.

The primary Israeli requirement of a political settlement would therefore be an authoritative Palestinian commitment to full peace (including normal diplomatic, cultural, and economic relations) and an unequivocal renunciation of all claims on Israel beyond those satisfied in the peace treaty itself through the establishment of an independent Palestinian state in the West Bank and Gaza. In addition to territorial claims, this renunciation would apply to property and repatriation claims. Indeed, a central feature of the treaty would have to be the liquidation of the whole refugee problem. Title to any remaining Israeli infrastructure in the West Bank and Gaza would pass to the Palestinian state and the Palestinians would declare that this constituted implementation of General Assembly Resolution 194 (III), thus signifying that the refugee problem had been resolved to their satisfaction. Israel, for its part, would then assume legal ownership of Arab property abandoned in 1948 as declared compensation for the property left by Jews in Arab countries after 1948, and announce its intention to press no further claims against those countries. Provisions for the establishment of a state of peace and the renunciation of further claims should be formally incorporated into a treaty in order to emphasize the finality of the settlement and obviate any rationale for subsequent revisionism, as might be implied by a different type of agreement, such as an armistice or a state of nonbelligerency.

Furthermore, the treaty would have to incorporate an agreement on Jerusalem guaranteeing the city's unity, and would also have to make some provision for Israel's economic interests. In general, the latter are not very extensive and are not threatened by withdrawal from the West Bank/Gaza (as has been argued above); they can probably be safeguarded by a formula similar to Article III.3 of the Egyptian-Israeli Peace Treaty, which includes a mutual obligation to terminate "economic boycotts and discriminatory barriers to the free movement of people and goods." However, the issue of water utilization demands more specific attention, and some limitation on Palestinian exploitation of the western subterranean aquifer, perhaps conditional on Israeli cooperation in overall water planning and conservation, should be an integral part of the settlement.

A second indispensable requirement is that Israel's other Arab neighbors be fully involved in the settlement. This implies, not only a verbal endorsement of the Israeli-Palestinian peace, but also participatory ratification, at least by Jordan, Saudi Arabia, Lebanon, and perhaps Syria—in addition to Egypt. Participatory ratification would mean peace agreements between these individual states and Israel and the establishment of normal bilateral relations as well as active involvement in the implementation of appropriate elements of the overall settlement (for example, financial support for the Palestinian state, rehabilitation of refugees not relocating to the West Bank or Gaza and elimination of UNRWA, dissolution of the PLO infrastructure outside the Palestinian state).

Finally, a Palestinian role in any possible future foreign military threat to Israel would have to be excluded through some limitation on Palestinian-Arab or Palestinian-Soviet military relations, and particularly by a ban on the stationing in or transit through Palestinian territory of foreign armies, even under the guise of military advisers. The most appropriate framework for such a ban would be a Palestinian agreement not to adhere to any military alliances or other joint-defense agreements, or to surrender any of its territory to another sovereign, it being clearly stipulated that should the Palestinian state cease to exist (as a result, perhaps, of some union with another Arab state), the provisions barring the introduction of other Arab or non-Arab armies would continue to apply to the West Bank and Gaza. In short, the Palestinian state would declare its military neutrality.[1]

Such an agreement would be an undeniable attenuation of future Palestinian sovereignty, even if freely assumed. However, it could be emphasized that neutrality would apply to the military sphere alone and need not entail complete political nonalignment; nor need it prevent the Palestinian state from maintaining special economic, religious, or cultural ties with other states or from participating in regional or international organizations. Except for membership in the Arab Collective Security Pact and the Joint Defense Council, for example, there is no reason why the Palestinian state could not belong to the Arab League or even provide the site of its headquarters. Despite the limitation on the principle of complete sovereign freedom, neutrality would therefore signify no real restrictions on Palestinian nonmilitary interests and might even confer substantial economic and security benefits. As a result, there is probably sufficient receptivity to the idea among Palestinians to make it feasible. Other Arab states might regret Palestinian neutrality as a missed opportunity to enlist an additional partner in their regional alignments. However, Palestinian neutrality could also be perceived as a benefit, insofar as it obviated a potential threat (especially to Jordan) and reduced the intensity of superpower competition for position in the Palestinian state. The most critical Arab states would therefore probably approach the question of Palestinian neutrality, at worst, with indifference, and at best, with positive enthusiasm.

From the Israeli perspective, an agreement on Palestinian military neutrality would not in and of itself prevent the movement of foreign armies into the West Bank and Gaza. However, violation of the agreement would constitute a clear and recognized casus belli, in the absence of which an Israeli decision to use force would be more constrained, if only for diplomatic considerations.

Political-military elements

Such an agreement would obviously have to be buttressed by monitoring procedures to provide early warning of threatening force movements toward Israel and the West Bank or Gaza. Furthermore, the existing force-limitation arrangements in Sinai should ideally be reproduced by an agreement with respect to the area east of the Jordan River. Taken together, these elements, along with Israeli diplomatic and commercial presence in Arab states, should give Israel a reasonable probability of sufficient warning time of an impending threat, and spare it the economic burden of a prolonged mobilization of reserves and the security risk of large standing Arab forces in close proximity to its vital core.

Monitoring procedures would essentially consist of Israeli observation and detection facilities (ground-based radars, optic and electronic sensors, other information-gathering facilities) in the Palestinian state, protected by Israeli personnel and with sufficient redundancy to accommodate technical breakdown. To reduce the threat of an attack from the east, Israel would also want to maintain in the West Bank a number of antiaircraft installations on the eastern crest of the mountain ridge, and the right to carry out overflights of a north-south corridor, at least until it is able to obtain a satellite observation system under its own control.

A combined assault of Eastern Front Arab armies across the Jordan River is likely to remain Israel's major strategic concern, and its need for early detection of an impending threat of this sort is widely recognized, even by some Palestinians who are otherwise uncompromising in their demands for Israeli withdrawal.[2] However, an observation capacity is also necessary to verify limitations on the military capacity of the Palestinian state itself.

It is most unlikely that a Palestinian state would constitute, in the foreseeable future, a serious independent military threat to Israel. It is true that Palestinian artillery could shell Israeli settlements and other targets. However, the actual threat to Israel would not be a function solely of the technical range of Palestinian guns (it is equally exposed, in this respect, to missile or air attack from much greater distances), but rather of the Palestinian calculation of probable consequences, beginning with Israeli counterfire and ending with massive retaliation. The most plausible danger, therefore, is that a Palestinian state would play a vanguard role in a coordinated Arab offensive. Palestinian forces, because of their potential proximity to Israeli communications facilities, road junctions, population centers, and airfields, could launch an artillery and missile barrage intended to interfere with Israeli mobilization of reserves and air force operations, while simultaneously seizing some Israeli frontier positions or at least fortifying the western Samarian foothills. Such actions would not immediately decide the outcome of a war, although they would certainly affect Israeli morale. But their most critical effect, if properly coordinated with the other Arab armies, might be to hamper an Israeli counteroffensive long enough for main-force units from the Eastern Front states, advancing even from relatively remote start-lines, to seize the central mountain ridge and then develop a final westward assault or, at the very least, impose an untenable political-strategic situation.

Such precise coordination would be difficult to achieve. The basic strategy itself might be politically unappealing to Palestinian decisionmakers, since the introduction of Arab armies into the West Bank would be a potential threat to Palestinian independence. Indeed, the memory of the consequences for the West Bank of Arab Legion involvement in the 1948 war against Israel, together with the prospect that the West Bank would bear much of the immediate physical brunt of combat, might be sufficient to deter Palestinian leaders from adopting any such strategy.

Nevertheless, the risk to Israel requires that Palestinian capacity to play a vanguard military role be minimized. This capacity could be altogether eliminated if the Palestinian state were completely demilitarized. Complete disarmament, however, is not feasible. A Palestinian state would require some armed forces, for at least two purposes. The first is as an attribute of sovereignty. Both the dignity of the state and the acceptability of the peace agreement would demand at least the universal symbolic evidence of independence.[3] Secondly, an internal security capability would be required to protect the regime, contain rejectionist and other sources of domestic disorder, and enforce the state's obligation not to permit acts of violence against neighboring states to originate from within its territory.

These objectives cannot be secured through disarmament, but they are consistent with certain limitations on force levels, weapons, and deployment that Israel would require. The major limitation would be on the size of the Palestinian army, which should consist of no more than three brigade-equivalents of motorized infantry, with appropriate support services but no brigade headquarters or reserves.[4] These forces could be equipped with armored reconnaissance vehicles, light mortars, and machine guns, but no tanks or missiles (ground-to-ground or ground-to-air) would be permitted. The army would be divided between the West Bank and Gaza in a ratio of two to one, and movement of forces or equipment between the two regions would require advance authorization by an Israeli military attaché or other liaison officer. The Palestinian navy, based in Gaza, would essentially be a coast guard and search and rescue force equipped with light patrol craft. The air force would also concentrate on search and rescue roles, and would be equipped with helicopters and light reconnaissance and transport craft, with perhaps one squadron of six to eight unarmed jet trainers for demonstration purposes. Aside from three to four helicopters stationed in Gaza, these aircraft would be based in Qalandiya, which would formally be a dual-purpose airport (civilian and military), but since the Palestinian air force would include no real combat aircraft, and since the airport would be under Israeli observation and within artillery range, this would result in no practical danger to Israel.

Aside from these limitations and a ban on fortifications, the other major constraint would be a prohibition on the development or importation of weapons of mass destruction, especially nuclear arms. If only because of the proximity of targets in Israel to Palestinian territory, and the uncontrollable immediate and long-term effects of such weapons, their use by a Palestinian state, even in the unlikely event that it managed to deploy them before Israel did, would be self-defeating, since even a "successful" first strike would, at a minimum, render the areas attacked inaccessible to Palestinians as well. Nevertheless, in this instance, unlike that of the conventional military balance, the risk of Palestinian miscalculation or irrationality would be so great, and the margin of Israeli error so small, that any Palestinian capability at all would be completely unacceptable, and precluded by treaty.

Compliance with the ban against heavy weapons and radioactive materials could be monitored by mixed Palestinian-Israeli civilian observation teams at land, sea, and air ports of entry. Limitations on indigenous production and deployment could be verified by aerial observation and electro-optic sensors.

Force limitations of this sort are an obvious derogation from unfettered Palestinian sovereignty and would probably arouse some resentment. Nevertheless, they would still permit a Palestinian state to maintain a military force that could satisfy symbolic and internal security needs, and there is some indirect evidence that military constraints, in principle if not in this specific format, may be acceptable.[5]

From Israel's perspective, a completely demilitarized Palestinian state would clearly be preferable, but the limitations suggested above, together with the strategic warning provided by Israeli diplomatic and commercial presence in the Palestinian and other Arab states, would almost certainly reduce the marginal military threat of a Palestinian state to tolerable levels.

Arms limitations would not, of course, eliminate the problem of terrorism emanating from the Palestinian state. It is necessary, however, to view this problem in perspective.

Despite the anguish it causes and the burdensome protective measures it has necessitated, terror does not constitute a strategic threat to Israel's basic national security. According to Israel Defense Forces' figures, the total number of civilians killed or wounded in terrorist attacks in Israel and the occupied territories since 1967 is less than the annual average number of traffic casualties.[6] In the aftermath of a settlement, Israeli civilians in the West Bank and Gaza would be less well protected, but they might also be less numerous, and their presence would be less provocative. More important, the collective Palestinian motivation to carry out or support terrorism against Israelis would diminish. Nevertheless, Palestinian ultras at least would view the "continuing struggle" as reason enough to undertake terrorist actions, and their freedom to operate in the West Bank and Gaza might actually increase after Israeli security services left. To cope with this danger, Israel would have to rely on defensive measures at home, its admittedly reduced intelligence capability in the West Bank and Gaza, and the capacity of the Palestinian state to prevent terrorist activities. If that state were itself indifferent or complicit, Israel could attempt to compel compliance through economic countermeasures (ranging from closure of its labor market to interference with West Bank/Gaza traffic), exercise of its reserved right of "hot pursuit," or retaliatory operations — all in accordance with circumstances, the magnitude of the problem, and expected effectiveness.

Spatial dimensions

Needless to say, Israeli security planners would prefer to reduce as much as possible the territory ultimately transferred to Palestinian rule. However, for reasons already discussed, the borders of a Palestinian state are likely to approximate the 1949 armistice lines, with the exception of a special arrangement for Jerusalem. At the same time, there are several reasons why it is important for Israel that the borders of the new state not coincide exactly with those of the West Bank and Gaza.

The first is political-psychological: to avoid a complete rollback of Israel to its previous physical configuration. Otherwise, the settlement could be portrayed as a unilateral Israeli withdrawal, rather than as a mutually acceptable agreement, thus detracting from its perceived finality and giving momentum to the hopes of Palestinian maximalists that it is just a stage in an ongoing process. The second reason is practical: the 1949 armistice lines include some striking human and physical anomalies resulting from the fortuitous positions of the contending armies at the time of the cease-fires. The most glaring of these anomalies could be eliminated without a major departure from the Green Line. Finally, the overall military risk of withdrawing from the West Bank can be partly mitigated by the retention of strategic locations close to the previous frontier.

Within the framework of "minor rectifications" or "border-straightening," two changes would appear to be of particular urgency for Israel (Map XI). The first is the annexation of the Latrun Salient, up to a line running approximately from Budrus through Giv'on and Bir Nabala to the northern limit of Jerusalem. Aside from keeping the new Jerusalem-Tel-Aviv highway under Israeli control (thus halving the travel time between the two cities required by the alternative route used between 1948 and 1967), this would broaden the Jerusalem Corridor and have the added advantage of permitting Israel to retain some of the settlements built in this area. The second requirement would be a southward extension, by about 10 kilometers, of the area of the Beisan Valley under Israeli sovereignty. The strategic rationale for this border change is that it would enable Israel to control the entrance to two of the axes (Mehola–Tayasir–Tubas and Tal Fass al-Jamal–Beqa'ot–Bayt 'Abd al-Qadir) leading up from the Jordan Valley to the Samarian mountains. Furthermore, it would increase Israel's ability to counterattack on the flank of an Eastern Front offensive developing farther south in the valley. It would also permit the retention of the two settlements (Shiloah and Mehola) in this area.

Beyond these indispensable changes, there are other, less extensive border alterations that could bring additional Jewish settlements under Israeli sovereignty.

It is possible that rectifications of this sort will be politically

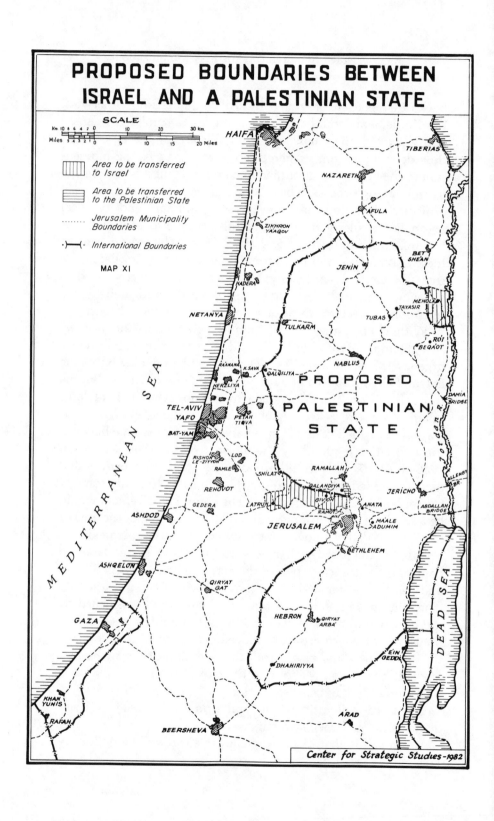

PROPOSED BOUNDARIES BETWEEN ISRAEL AND A PALESTINIAN STATE

SCALE

Km 10 8 6 4 2 0   10   20   30 Km.
Miles 5 4 3 2 1 0   5   10   15   20 Miles

▦   Area to be transferred to Israel

▤   Area to be transferred to the Palestinian State

....   Jerusalem Municipality Boundaries

·)—I—(·   International Boundaries

MAP XI

HAIFA

TIBERIAS

NAZARETH

AFULA

ZIKHRON YAAQOV

BET SHEAN

JENIN

HADERA

MEHOLA
TAYASIR

NETANYA

TULKARM

TUBAS

ROI
BEQA'OT

RAANANA   K.SAVA
QALQILIYA

NABLUS

HERZLIYA

PROPOSED

DAMIA BRIDGE

TEL-AVIV YAFO

PETAH TIQVA

PALESTINIAN

BAT-YAM

STATE

RISHON LE-ZIYYON   LOD

RAMLE

SHILAT

RAMALLAH

REHOVOT

QALANDIYA

JERICHO

ALLENBY BR.

GEDERA

LATRUN

GIVON
RAMOT

ANATA

ABDALLAH BRIDGE

ASHDOD

JERUSALEM

MAALE ADUMIM

BETHLEHEM

ASHQELON

QIRYAT GAT

HEBRON   QIRYAT ARBA'

GAZA

EIN GEDDI

DHAHIRIYYA

DEAD SEA

KHAN YUNIS

RAFAH

ARAD

BEERSHEVA

MEDITERRANEAN SEA

Jordan R.

Center for Strategic Studies-1982

unattainable without some element of reciprocity. If that is the case, Israel could, as an additional border-straightening measure, transfer to the Palestinian state some of the Arab-populated towns and villages now on the Israeli side of the Green Line.

If individuals potentially affected by these land transfers were given a choice of coming under a new sovereignty or receiving equitable compensation and relocating within the previous jurisdiction, the human disruption would be limited, especially since most would probably prefer to remain where they are. In terms of Israel's national security and other concerns, this dimension of the peace formula is less than ideal, but it does confer some advantages (including a measure of population homogenization), salvages some significant interests, and further reduces the risks of withdrawal. In the overall context of a settlement, it therefore constitutes a cost that is not disproportionate to the benefits.

Temporal dimensions

In addition to substantive requirements, Israel must also consider the manner of implementation most likely to reinforce the stability and durability of the peace settlement. An immediate and simultaneous implementation of all its provisions would deny opportunities for resistance or targets of subversion to opponents of the peace in both camps, and might constitute a greater psychological contribution to reconciliation between the various parties. On the other hand, it is quite unlikely that any political solution will allow the accumulated hostility and distrust to disappear instantaneously, and the need to test the viability of the settlement and to build confidence indicates that the agreement should be implemented over time, as was the Egyptian-Israeli peace treaty. Furthermore, the multiplicity of actors and the greater complexity of the issues argue in favor of a somewhat longer transition period than in the Egyptian-Israeli case.

Any transition period is to some extent arbitrary and unreliable, since the real criterion for continued implementation should be, not the passage of a specified number of years, but the fulfillment of certain conditions, and fulfillment can theoretically be reversed once any transition period, regardless of its duration, has expired. Nevertheless, a transition period must be defined in terms of time as well. Otherwise, there is no reasonable prospect that temporary arrangements will end and that the provisions of a permanent settlement will be carried out.[7] The transition period should therefore be short enough to have a visible time horizon, but it must also be long enough for commitments to be tested with some measure of confidence.

A five-to-ten-year period would appear to meet these criteria. At the beginning of this period, once a functioning regime had come into existence, Israeli armed forces would be transferred to areas designated as transitional security zones — the Jordan Valley, Ma'ale Adumim (with an access road, perhaps through Anata), and the southern Gaza Strip between Rafah and Khan Yunis. Existing settlements in these zones would be maintained, but no new ones would be erected without permission from the Palestinian government. At the same time, any of the smaller outposts whose dismantling has been agreed upon during negotiations would be relocated to Israel. The rest — apart from those to be included in Israel or in the security zones — would then pass to Palestinian jurisdiction.

The transition period itself would serve to verify the implementation of the overall agreement. During this period, Israel would be particularly concerned about a number of vital indicators: the general state of Israeli-Palestinian relations, the level of terrorist activity (if any) and official Palestinian involvement, the condition of Jews living under Palestinian rule, the liquidation of UNRWA and the absorption of refugees into the Palestinian state, the nature of Israel's relations with other Arab states, the elimination of PLO infrastructure in those states, the naturalization and rehabilitation of Palestinian refugees preferring to remain in those states, and the potential Arab security threat, as reflected in defense expenditures and military inventories of the various Arab states. If these indicators suggested, toward the end of the transition period, that the peace process was well entrenched and as self-perpetuating as the fundamental character of international relations allows, Israel would withdraw its armed forces inside the permanent boundary. If technological developments permitted, it would also remove its monitoring facilities, or else operate them jointly with Palestinian forces, and stop exercising its overflight rights. At this point, the implementation phase of the settlement would be completed and the peoples of the region might be able to turn their attention to different challenges and rewards.

7

The Calculus of Decision

Whenever security is at issue, there exists a natural inclination to prefer the status quo to any alternative. This choice is often perceived as a choice between the known and the unknown. Considered in these terms, the tendency "to err on the side of caution" is readily comprehensible. The underlying perception, however, is false. An immediate reality may indeed be more knowable than any hypothetical alternative, but an evaluation of the potential future consequences for national security of that reality is subject to the same uncertainties as is an evaluation of the implications of the alternatives. A policy aimed at perpetuating the status quo is not automatically the most prudent strategy for any state to pursue; it can be so judged only after a comparative analysis of the probable overall value of the various alternatives has been attempted.

Israeli policy

In the present case, the analysis suggests that the status quo, despite its geomilitary advantages, implies great diplomatic, economic, demographic, and moral costs and risks, which are furthermore likely to grow rather than to diminish with the passage of time. Nevertheless, the status quo remains preferable to nonterritorial settlements, which, even if attainable, would almost surely have a devastating effect on the character, and perhaps the very viability, of an independent Jewish state. With respect to an Israeli-Palestinian settlement that circumvented the

PLO, its durability (as long as the PLO retains its Arab and international standing) would not appear to be great, and the costs and potential risk of breakdown make this alternative, too, strategically inferior to the status quo, although to a somewhat lesser degree. On the other hand, an Israeli-Arab settlement that bypassed the Palestinians completely could, under optimal conditions, be more sustainable; the most logical variant of such a settlement — a federal state in Jordan — might actually be somewhat preferable, from Israel's perspective, to the status quo.

However, the assessment of the implications of a PLO-controlled Palestinian state suggests that while its immediate costs are similar to those of a solution not involving the PLO or other Palestinians, its potential risks can be more readily foreseen and contained in the settlement process, and its potential benefits are considerably greater. Therefore, a settlement on this basis would probably leave Israel in a better overall position than would a continuing political stalemate or any of the other potential outcomes.

Furthermore, this goal should be sought on an urgent basis. Delay merely increases the physical obstacles to and material costs of a change of course and renders the present course progressively less reversible, if only for domestic political reasons. Meanwhile, the burdens of the status quo will also continue to grow, perhaps to the point where Israel's ability to secure through negotiations all the risk- and cost-minimization provisions essential to protect its interests would be adversely affected. In that case, the political-strategic value to Israel of a Palestine-state settlement would diminish, without producing any countervailing enhancement in the value of other alternatives, and the overall consequence would be an even crueler and more restricted range of policy options.

Implications for Israeli military posture

Israeli agreement to an independent Palestinian state is intended to remove the main motif of Israeli-Arab conflict and diminish the political basis of Arab threats to Israeli security. If this state were created with appropriate risk-minimization provisions for Israel and within the context of a broad Israeli-Arab détente, it would probably result in a significantly less tense and dangerous environment for Israel.

It is unlikely, however, that this political transformation would permit an immediate easing of the Israeli defense burden. Until more relaxed Arab-Israeli relations were reflected in the reconfiguration of Arab armies, Israel would still have to maintain large standing forces. Furthermore, the redeployment of Israeli facilities and equipment from the territories into Israel itself would entail large (if one-time) costs. Only after the termination of the Arab-Israeli conflict had become a normal feature of the Middle Eastern landscape would substantial reductions in Israeli force levels and defense expenditures be feasible.

Even then, the same measures necessary to lower political tensions would have produced a more "nervous" military doctrine in Israel. Despite limitations on Palestinian military capacity and the retention of Israeli early-warning facilities in the West Bank, the inevitable effect of withdrawal would be a loss of strategic depth and topographic advantage and a reduced margin of error, hence, an even greater Israeli intolerance of ambiguity. More than ever, Israel would therefore be compelled to resort to anticipatory action in the face of potential military dangers, and particularly to preempt threatening developments or movements east of the Jordan River by resuming military control of the West Bank.

Paradoxically, then, a more stable political regime in the region would result in a less stable Arab-Israeli military balance, dictated as much by geography as by technology. In less delicate terms, continuing Palestinian independence would be a permanent hostage to nonthreatening Arab behavior.

Palestinians and other Arabs would undoubtedly find this situation uncomfortable, but it would hardly be ideal from Israel's perspective either. Any possibility of making Israeli-Arab relations less sensitive to misperception—by adopting confidence-building measures such as prior notification and routine observation of military maneuvers, for example—should therefore be pursued. Nevertheless, since the physical separation of forces could not be replicated in the east on the same scale as in Sinai, a fairly low threshold for Israeli military preemption would be virtually foreordained.

Implications for western powers

The overall effect of a Palestine-state settlement on vital Israeli interests has been assessed in terms of measured optimism. An even more restrained evaluation of its impact on western interests is called for. For Israel, a settlement of the Arab-Israeli conflict would touch directly on its central dilemma; for the western powers, it might, if achieved, eliminate only one among a number of challenges — and not necessarily the most critical — to their interests in the region.

The western world, with the United States as its foremost component, has two essential requirements of the Middle East/Persian Gulf region: that access to its mineral resources be reasonably secure, and that the region (for geopolitical as well as economic reasons) not fall under the domination of the Soviet Union or any other hostile force. These requirements are threatened by a variety of factors — hostile or extortionate local governments, interstate conflicts, domestic instability fueled by ethnic, religious, economic, or ideological tensions, Soviet military power, and even western disunity and inconstant political will. An Arab-Israeli settlement, in general, and the creation of a Palestinian state, in particular, would have virtually no impact on domestic or other interstate sources of instability, or on the political determination of the West to resist Soviet encroachment (or unreasonable demands from local governments). Nor would it assure western strategic access to the region, since an overt foreign presence in Arab countries is rejected even now for reasons not confined to western identification with Israel. Therefore, western expectations of a golden age of regional tranquility and Arab-western cooperation in the aftermath of an Arab-Israeli settlement would soon clash with some less pleasant realities.

On the other hand, such a settlement would eliminate one

focus of anti-American sentiment in the Arab world and make it easier for Arab governments so inclined to resist Soviet blandishments. Furthermore, political measures that reduce the probability of another Arab-Israeli war are ipso facto desirable, if only because they remove a potential strain in the western alliance and reduce the risk of a direct Soviet-American confrontation. An Arab-Israeli settlement, while insufficient to secure western interests, would therefore be a positive development meriting western support.

However, excessive zeal based on belief in the desirability of *any* settlement is liable to be misplaced, and even counterproductive. For western support, especially if it takes the form of pressure on Israel to concede some of its risk-minimization requirements or to accept third-party substitutes for Palestinian and Arab undertakings, may harden Palestinian-Arab demands by strengthening their perception that their bargaining position had improved, and thus undermine the prospect that a mutually acceptable settlement could be reached. Alternatively, and perhaps even more dangerously, western impatience might lead to a settlement that would be structurally and/or psychologically vulnerable to subsequent breakdown. In that case, even the marginal western benefits from a Palestinian state would prove to be ephemeral.

Any western involvement in the process should therefore concentrate on postsettlement material support, and be clearly complementary to the main effort: bilateral negotiations aimed at producing an agreement as self-enforcing as possible. With respect to the most critical western actor — the United States — this would entail involvement of two sorts. The first would be a commitment to participate in the economic consolidation of the Palestinian state, in order to reduce the risk of revisionism stemming from domestic discontent there. The second would be a commitment to a more intimate and institutionalized Israeli-American strategic relationship.

In operational terms, this would mean cooperation in defense production and research-and-development, intelligence sharing, provision of the most advanced reconnaissance and early-warning equipment (especially satellite systems), joint contingency planning, and long-term assistance programs not subject to the vagaries of annual authorization — all this geared to Israel's most proximate concerns, as well as to more remote, extraregional threats. Symbolically, this American commitment would be important in order to overcome the sense of insecurity in Israel associated with territorial constriction. Practically, it would be vital in order to provide political, economic, and technological compensation to Israel for the geomilitary sacrifices required by a double-track strategy.

Procedural considerations

Questions of bargaining tactics, venue, composition of negotiating teams, legal implications with respect to the Israeli-Egyptian Peace Treaty, and so forth are best left to experts on such subjects. There are, however, some procedural matters that bear so directly on the prospects for settlement that they fall within the purview of strategic analysis.

One of these is the potential contribution of intermediaries. The enormous hostility and mutual suspicion between Israelis and Palestinians may mean that the psychological barriers to productive negotiations, or to the mere agreement to negotiate, could not be surmounted without the involvement of a third party. If this is so, then the services of an intermediary, of proven discretion and reliability to both sides, might be sought out. The function of this intermediary would be to make initial contacts, provide "good offices" and facilitate the beginning of negotiations, rather than to assume an active mediating role. At a much more advanced stage, the same party might help to codify and implement technical agreements otherwise threatened by the emotional legacies of the conflict.

A related matter is the question of whether an Israeli-PLO agreement should be pursued openly or in secret. For Israel, the temptations of a public approach are considerable. Most alluring of these is the prospect that an open declaration of readiness to discuss with the PLO the establishment of an independent Palestinian state would immediately improve Israel's standing in the international community. Secondly, it would force the PLO as a whole to confront the true implications of its rejectionist ideology, and thus might possibly lead to the discreditation or disintegration of that organization. In addition, if the PLO's strength, reputation, and recognized position as the Palestinians' "sole legitimate spokesman" should change sufficiently to make solutions not involving the PLO more inherently attractive to Israel, an open approach might also induce other potential interlocutors (West Bank and Gaza Palestinians or Jordan) to come forward, perhaps on even more accommodating terms, for fear of altogether missing an opportunity to secure Israeli withdrawal.[1]

The drawbacks of public diplomacy, however, are almost certainly even weightier. The public relations advantage to Israel, for example, would probably prove to be very short-lived. Many western powers have long been inclined toward this kind of settlement and have been restrained from promoting it even more vigorously precisely because of Israel's uncompromising posture. Once this basic obstacle were removed, the immediate flood of approval would soon be followed by a growing impatience to see the prospective deal consummated. Israel, having already conceded the principle, would come under increasing pressure to show flexibility on details — details which, though of fundamental importance to Israeli security, would be seen by other parties as minor irritants in the way of a settlement. Even the United States, despite clear reasons to act otherwise, might feel compelled to join in the chorus condemning Israeli "intransigence." In the end, Israel might eventually be compelled to accept a poor and dangerous settlement; but even if it were able to resist, the potential improvement in its international standing would have meanwhile been transformed into further deterioration.

Just as daunting is the probable impact of publicity on the prospects of achieving any settlement at all. Premature disclosure that negotiations were taking place, or merely contemplated, would seriously constrain the ability of each side to negotiate productively, and might completely abort the negotiations. Domestic pressure would be so intense that the required retreat from current positions, even the very act of negotiating, might be politically impossible. Public ratification — constitutionally and otherwise — of the results of a successful negotiation would naturally be required, as would the participatory involvement of the major Arab states and the United States; Israel would not implement an agreement until reasonably confident that the capacity of rejectionists to subvert it ex post facto had been eliminated. But it is unlikely that negotiations could be successful, or even take place, unless they were shielded from the harmful glare of publicity.

If Israel decided to pursue such a settlement, not as an exercise in public relations, but as a serious policy objective, it could create a more propitious prenegotiation atmosphere by declaring a suspension of new settlement activity in the territories or refining, perhaps in the context of autonomy discussions, the vague recognition it accorded at Camp David to "the legitimate rights of the Palestinians." Such declarations might enhance the willingness or ability of PLO leaders to respond to a concrete Israeli initiative. And if subsequent developments were encouraging, measures to prepare public opinion on both sides, such as a moratorium on PLO violence and permission for deportees identified with the PLO to return to the West Bank or Gaza, would ease resistance to later, more dramatic disclosures.

But the initiative itself should be unpublicized. And with respect to any actual negotiations — their progress or their very existence — Israel should insist on secrecy, while reserving an option of "plausible deniability" if the secrecy is breached too soon. In that case, the effort could be deferred until more auspicious conditions permitted a resumption of the search for peace.

The pursuit of a settlement with the PLO leading to an independent Palestinian state, with appropriate risk-minimization provisions, would best promote Israel's fundamental strategic objectives of neutralizing the Palestine issue as a factor in Israeli-Arab relations and reducing the overall Arab threat to Israeli security, while preserving the Jewish, democratic character and vitality of Israeli society. Such a settlement would not be a panacea for all of Israel's problems; it would not provide absolute security or guarantee perpetual peace. But given Israel's historical and geographical circumstances, no conceivable posture is without considerable risks and costs. This one, however, is almost surely the "least of all evils." Rather than avoiding a comprehensive peace with the Palestinians, Israel should therefore pursue the Palestine-state settlement as the primary goal of its foreign and national security policy.

Notes
Bibliography
Index

Notes

1. Introduction

1. The Palestinian National Covenant, adopted by the founding congress of the PLO in 1964 and amended in 1968, remains the basic official expression of the Palestinian movement's objectives and perceptions. The Covenant unconditionally rejects Israel's right to exist and opposes any compromise with the goal of total liberation. This world view pervades the entire document but is most concisely stated in Article 21: "The Palestinian Arab people . . . rejects every solution that is a substitute for a complete liberation of Palestine, and rejects all plans that aim at the settlement of the Palestine issue or its internationalization." Text in John Norton Moore, ed., *The Arab-Israeli Conflict*, vol. III, *Documents* (Princeton: Princeton University Press, 1974), pp. 705–711. It is especially important to note that *Fatah*, the dominant element within the PLO and the one portrayed by Arab and western observers as most moderate, is no less uncompromising in its strategic posture than the so-called "extremist" movements. In its Fourth Conference, convened in May 1980 after a lapse of nine years, *Fatah* once again stressed its devotion to the total liberation of Palestine and the complete liquidation of "the Zionist entity" — economically, politically, militarily, socially, and ideologically — and repudiated all solutions that deviated from these goals. See the political communiqué of the *Fatah* conference, especially sections 8, 9, and 11, in *al-Liwa'* (Beirut), June 2, 1980.

2. In June 1974, the twelfth session of the Palestine National Council adopted a ten-point program that called for the establishment of a "militant, independent National Authority (*sulta wataniyya*) of the people on all parts of Palestinian territory that will be liberated" (Resolution 2) but tied this "concession" to a rejection of "recognition,

reconciliation, secure borders, abandonment of the historic right and depriving our people of their rights to return" (Resolution 3) and pledged that the independent national authority would "struggle for the unification of the front-line countries in order to complete the liberation of all Palestinian soil" (Resolution 7). *Arab Report and Record* (London), 11 (1–15 June 1974), 239. The thirteenth PNC session in March 1977 defined the national authority as an "independent national state" (Resolution 11), but otherwise left intact its rejectionist posture. *Arab Report and Record*, 6 (16–31 March 1977), 236.

2. Israel's Security Dilemma

1. Israel's economic development in this period is summarized in Nadav Safran, *Israel: The Embattled Ally* (Cambridge, Mass.: Harvard University Press, 1978), chap. 8, especially pp. 108–111.

2. In the period 1968–1972, gross fixed domestic capital formation more than doubled, in real terms. However, this overstates, to some extent, the impact on productive capacity, especially for export, since residential housing during this period grew from 25 percent to almost 40 percent of total investment. Israel, Central Bureau of Statistics, *Statistical Abstract of Israel*, no. 29 (1978), table vi/6, pp. 172–173 (hereafter cited as *Statistical Abstract*).

3. Ibid., table vii/5, pp. 206–207.

4. Yehoshua Raviv, *The Arab-Israeli Military Balance*, Center for Strategic Studies Paper 7 (Tel-Aviv, 1980).

5. Total regular forces amount to about 175,000 men and women, and reserves (almost all men) number some 365,000. Mark A. Heller, ed., *The Middle East Military Balance* (Tel-Aviv: Center for Strategic Studies, forthcoming). Average reserve duty is approximately one month per year (somewhat more for officers), meaning that 1/12 of the reserves — about 30,000 men — are doing reserve duty at any given time. Thus, total forces-in-being are approximately 205,000, of which 175–185,000 are men, that is, over 23 percent of the 767,100 Jewish males aged eighteen to fifty-four. This percentage should be reduced somewhat to take account of non-Jewish Israelis serving in the Israel Defense Forces. Population figures taken from *Statistical Abstract*, no. 32 (1981), table ii/18, p. 52.

6. Total foreign debt at the end of 1980 was $21.88 billion, of which $11.3 billion was governmental or Bank of Israel debt. Ibid., table vii/5, pp. 198–199.

7. In the period 1974–1980, total growth in GNP per capita was 2.56 percent, which is equivalent to an average annual growth of about 0.4 percent. Computed from ibid., table vi/2, p. 165.

8. For a more detailed analysis of the geomilitary importance of the West Bank see Aryeh Shalev, *The West Bank: Line of Defense* (Tel-Aviv: Hakibbutz Hameuhad, 1982) (Hebrew).

9. Between 1951 and 1955, over 400 Israelis were killed by Palestinian *fida'iyyun* operating from the Gaza Strip. Martin Gilbert, *The Arab-Israeli Conflict: Its History in Maps* (London: Weidenfeld and Nicholson, 1974), p. 60.

3. Implications of Alternatives to a Palestinian State

1. For more details on the Arab buildup since 1973 see Yehoshua Raviv, *The Arab-Israeli Military Balance*, Center for Strategic Studies Paper 7 (Tel-Aviv, 1980).

2. Palestinian disillusionment with their reception in the Arab world is vividly described, inter alia, in Rosemary Sayigh, *Palestinians: From Peasants to Revolutionaries* (London: Zed Press, 1979), chaps. 3–4; Yehoshafat Harkabi, "The Palestinians in the Fifties and Their Awakening as Reflected in Their Literature," in Moshe Maoz, ed., *Palestinian Arab Politics* (Jerusalem: Jerusalem Academic Press, 1975); and Naseer H. Aruri and Samih Farsoun, "Palestinian Communities in Arab Host Countries," in Khalil Nakhleh and Elia Zureik, eds., *The Sociology of the Palestinians* (London: Croom Helm, 1980), chap. 5. One writer ascribes the consolidation of Palestinian nationalism directly to the mistreatment of Palestinians by Arab regimes and their rejection by Arab masses. W.F. Abboushi, "Changing Political Attitudes in the West Bank After Camp David," in *A Palestinian Agenda for the West Bank and Gaza*, ed. Emile A. Nakhleh, American Enterprise Institute Study 277 (Washington, 1980), pp. 11–12.

3. For an elaboration on this theme see Walid Khalidi, "Thinking the Unthinkable: A Sovereign Palestinian State," *Foreign Affairs*, 56 (July 1978), 695–697.

4. The leader of the Shi'a-based *'Amal* movement, Nabih Berri, explained his support for Palestinian armed presence in southern Lebanon by arguing that "the Palestinian rifle" seeks to establish a Palestinian state and the return of the Palestinians to their land. If that struggle were abandoned, the result would be "implantation," that is,

permanent settlement of the Palestinians in Lebanon. Interview in *Monday Morning* (Beirut), April 1–7, 1982.

5. See, for example, the interview with Phalangist leader Bashir Jumayyil, *Al-Anwar* (Beirut), September 21, 1980.

6. For more on the nature of the linkage see Avi Plascov, "The 'Palestinian Gap' Between Israel and Egypt," *Survival*, 22 (March–April 1980).

7. In his speech to the Israeli Knesset, Sadat emphasized that he sought a just and durable peace based on "complete withdrawal from Arab territories occupied after 1967" and the right of the Palestinian people "to self-determination including their right to establish their own state." Text printed in the *New York Times*, November 21, 1977.

8. In the "Framework for Peace in the Middle East Agreed at Camp David," signed on September 17, 1978, Israel and Egypt agreed to begin negotiations, not later than three years after the establishment of a self-governing authority in the West Bank and Gaza, to determine the final status of these territories. According to section A.1(c) of this agreement, the solution must "recognize the legitimate rights of the Palestinian people and their just requirements." Text printed in United States, Department of State, *The Camp David Summit*, Publication 8954 (Washington, 1978), p. 8. The adherence of Israel and Egypt to the "Framework" agreement is reaffirmed in the preamble to the peace treaty of March 26, 1979, and in the joint letter of Sadat and Prime Minister Begin to President Carter of the same date. Text in the *New York Times*, March 27, 1979.

9. Some 100 Egyptian lawyers demonstrated against the peace treaty and burned Israeli flags to mark the first anniversary of the exchange of ambassadors between Israel and Egypt. *Jerusalem Post*, February 27, 1981.

10. For more details on VAT-related manifestations see Elie Rekhess and Dan Avidan, "The West Bank and Gaza Strip," in *Middle East Contemporary Survey*, ed. Colin Legum, vol. I: 1976–77 (New York and London: Holmes and Meier, 1978), pp. 292–293; and *Jerusalem Post*, December 3, 4, 6, 7, and 8, 1981. The Jerusalem District Electricity Company controversy is discussed in the *Jerusalem Post*, January 11, 1980; *Ma'ariv* (Tel-Aviv), January 23, 1980; and *Jerusalem Post*, January 13 and February 17, 1981. A letter of clarification from the chairman of the company's board of directors, Anwar Nusaybah, also appears in the *Jerusalem Post*, on January 25, 1981. The politicization of the West Bank teachers' strike is described in the *Jerusalem Post*, February 3 and March 1 and 11, 1981.

11. See, for example, Ya'acov Talmon, "The Homeland Is in Danger: An Open Letter to the Historian Menachem Begin," *Ha'aretz* (Tel-Aviv), March 31, 1980; statement by Labor party chairman Shimon Peres, *Jerusalem Post*, March 29, 1982.

12. On this point see Amnon Rubinstein, "A Touch of Shame," *Ha'aretz*, September 3, 1981. The political impact of demographic change may be felt long before numerical parity is reached. Parity, however, provides a salient watershed and various attempts have been made to forecast the year in which the Jewish-Arab balance in mandatory Palestine will tip in favor of the latter. A recent, highly detailed example is Moshe Hartman, *Jewish and Arab Population in Eretz Yisrael: The Year 2000*, Tel-Aviv University Project on Criteria for Defining Secure Borders (Tel-Aviv, n.d.) (Hebrew). Hartman's forecasts are based on certain assumptions about projected rates of natural increase, Arab population movements, and net Jewish immigration. If net Jewish immigration is zero, parity is expected around 1995. If average net Jewish immigration is 25,000 per year, parity will be delayed, mutatis mutandis, by approximately ten years. (Table 3, p. 15.) The latter assumption, once thought to be conservative, now appears quite optimistic. In 1974–1978, average net annual Jewish immigration was 9,000. "Setting the Record Straight on Emigration," *Jerusalem Post*, March 24,1980. In 1979 and 1980, emigration actually exceeded immigration by about 10,000 each year and the projected balance for 1981 is also negative, by about 9,000. *Jerusalem Post*, December 11, 1981. On the other hand, large-scale Arab emigration may continue, as it has done in the past, to neutralize the impact of the higher Arab rate of natural increase.

13. For more on patterns of employment in Israel see Chapter 5.

14. "A Lasting Peace in the Middle East: An American View," address by Secretary of State William P. Rogers, December 9, 1969, in United States Information Service, *United States Foreign Policy— Middle East: Basic Documents, 1950–1973* (Tel-Aviv, n.d.), p.41.

15. "News Conference, March 24," *Department of State Bulletin*, 78 (May 1978), 25.

16. An overview of the evolution of American policy toward the Palestinians in recent years is presented in two Center for Strategic Studies papers by Abraham Ben-Zvi, *The United States and the Palestinians: The Carter Era* (Tel-Aviv, 1981), and *The Reagan Presidency and the Palestinian Predicament: An Interim Analysis* (Tel-Aviv, 1982). Like other foreign policy questions to which the United States itself is not a direct party, this one is probably not of intense concern to most Americans, and

public opinion in general does not yet propel the government in any particular direction. It is interesting to note, however, that a Harris poll in the fall of 1980 revealed that over 70 percent of Americans were in favor of an independent Palestinian state in the West Bank, even though a majority also rejected the PLO as a valid interlocutor. *Ma'ariv*, October 3, 1980.

17. For some variations on his own theme see Yigal Allon, "Israel: The Case for Defensible Borders," *Foreign Affairs*, 55 (October 1976); "The West Bank and Gaza Within the Framework of a Middle East Peace Settlement," *Middle East Review*, 12 (Winter 1979–80); and "Anatomy of Autonomy," *Jerusalem Post International Edition*, June 3–9, 1979, p. 8.

18. See, for example, Moshe Dayan, "After All, What About the Mountain Ridge?" *Yedi'ot Aharonot* (Tel-Aviv), February 13, 1981.

19. Allon, "The West Bank and Gaza," p. 17, and "Anatomy of Autonomy."

20. The Labor party's preelection conference was held in two sessions: the first in December 1980, the second in February 1981. Its resolutions served as the party's electoral platform. In the political chapter, the party declared that "autonomy" was viewed as a transitional arrangement that should not stand in the way of a final settlement based on "territorial compromise and "defensible borders." Labor's view of "defensible borders," to the extent that it is uniform, can be inferred from Chapter 20, which states: "During implementation of the autonomy, complete Israeli control will continue in the security zones, in which IDF forces will be deployed and which will include the Jerusalem area and settlement zones in the Jordan Valley (including the northwest Dead Sea), the Etzion Bloc, and the southern Gaza Strip. The status and continued development of Israeli settlements in these zones will be guaranteed." Israel Labor Party, *Resolutions of the Third Party Conference* (Tel-Aviv, 1981), p. 10 (Hebrew).

21. The Summit Conference communiqué called for "just peace based on complete Israeli withdrawal from the territories conquered in 1967, including Arab Jerusalem, and the assurance of the inalienable national rights of the Palestinian people and the establishment of its independent state on the soil of its homeland." "Radio Amman," November 5, 1978 (text in Israel, Ministry for Foreign Affairs, Center for Research and Political Planning, *Document 22/78*, November 6, 1978).

22. *New York Times*, November 21, 1977.

23. See, for example, Husayn's speech to the Conference of Arab

Foreign and Economics Ministers in July 1980. "Radio Amman," July 6, 1980 (text in US, Foreign Broadcast Information Service, *Daily Report: Middle East and Africa*, V, no. 133, July 9, 1980, pp. A1-A4).

24. "Meetings with Arab Kings Described in Dayan's New Book," *Jerusalem Post*, March 1, 1981.

25. Thomas C. Schelling, *The Strategy of Conflict* (Oxford: Oxford University Press, 1960), p. 57.

26. Ibid., pp. 68–69.

27. For some specific suggestions see Chapter 6.

28. The Middle East as a whole is divided along lines of language, religion, or some other determinant of collective identity. In Palestine itself there are, in addition to Jews and Arabs (Muslims and Christians of various denominations), numerous Circassians and a fairly substantial Druze population.

29. Among Israeli political figures, the case for "functional partition" was espoused most consistently by Moshe Dayan. It is vigorously advocated at the unofficial level by the Jerusalem Institute for Federal Studies, whose moving spirit is Daniel J. Elazar.

30. The range of possible variations is suggested in Daniel J. Elazar and Ira Sharkansky, *Alternative Federal Solutions to the Problem of the Administered Territories* (Jerusalem: Jerusalem Institute for Federal Studies, 1978); Daniel J. Elazar, *The Camp David Framework for Peace: A Shift Toward Shared Rule*, American Enterprise Institute Study 236 (Washington, 1979); and Daniel J. Elazar and others, *Israel, the Palestinians, and the Territories: Some Alternative Frameworks for Peace* (Jerusalem: Jerusalem Institute for Federal Studies, 1981).

31. See, for example, the statement by Prime Minister Begin that "there will never again be a border in the western part of the land of Israel," *New York Times*, May 4, 1979; and the assertion by Interior Minister Yosef Burg (who is also head of the Israeli delegation to the autonomy negotiations) that Israel sees the autonomy as "an alternative" to a Palestinian state, *Jerusalem Post*, November 10, 1981.

32. An inventory of existing forms of self-rule or autonomy surveyed combinations of self-rule and shared rule in fifty-two states. The incidence of civil strife and violence in these states seems to be directly related to the degree of population heterogeneity. Where ethnic, religious, or linguistic minorities are small, dispersed, or nonexistent, violence has been minimal. Where the population is more evenly divided, and especially where different groups have been concentrated in different parts of the state, secessionist violence has been more pronounced. Many of the most prolonged and bloody cases of domestic

conflict—Lebanon, Cyprus, Sudan—are actually found in the Middle East region. Daniel J. Elazar, *Arrangements for Self-Rule and Autonomy in Various Countries of the World: A Preliminary Inventory* (Jerusalem: Jerusalem Institute for Federal Studies, 1978).

33. For more on the "third force" see Mark Heller, "Voices from the West Bank," *Moment* (Boston), 3 (April 1978), 25–29, 52–53; and "The Vulnerability of the Third Force," *Leviathan* (Boston), 2 (Spring 1978), 28–33.

34. Local developments in the wake of the Sadat initiative are described in Dan Avidan and Elie Rekhess, "The West Bank and Gaza Strip," in *Middle East Contemporary Survey*, ed. Colin Legum, vol.II: 1977–78 (New York and London: Holmes and Meier, 1979), pp. 288–292; and Yehuda Litani, "Leadership in the West Bank and Gaza," *The Jerusalem Quarterly*, no. 14 (Winter 1980), 99–109.

35. For a brief overview of earlier approaches to home-rule in the territories see Mark Heller, "Begin's False Autonomy," *Foreign Policy*, no. 37 (Winter 1979–80), 115–116, and "Politics and Social Change in the West Bank Since 1967," in *Palestinian Society and Politics*, ed. Joel S. Migdal (Princeton: Princeton University Press, 1980), pp. 200–201.

36. The vulnerability of potential interlocutors from within the territories to charges of cowardice, corruption, or worse is explained in an interview with Anwar Nusaybah in *Migvan* (Tel-Aviv), no. 57 (March 1981), 22–24.

37. Khalidi, "Thinking the Unthinkable," p. 698.

38. In 1978, President Sadat suggested as an interim measure that the West Bank revert to Jordan and the Gaza Strip to Egypt, and explained his proposal as an effort to facilitate Israel's withdrawal. "I want," he said, "to make it easy for Mr. Begin." *New York Times*, May 11, 1978.

39. See *al-Majalla* (London), April 11, 1981.

40. *Al-Majalla*, April 26, 1980.

41. To justify his campaign for a political solution, al-Hasan emphasized these advantages on several occasions. See, for example, interviews in *al-Ra'i al-'Amm* (Kuwait), April 15, 1980, and *al-Nahar al-'Arabi wa'l Dawli* (Paris), October 26, 1980. Nevertheless, he was subjected to a stinging attack by the rejectionist organizations, especially the Popular Front for the Liberation of Palestine—General Command. See *ila l'Amam* (Beirut), April 25, 1980.

42. For examples of rejection of the Jordanian option by King Husayn, see his statement on "Radio Amman," January 7, 1981, and interviews in *Monday Morning*, December 22, 1980, *The Sunday Times*

(London), January 18, 1981, and *Newsweek*, March 23, 1981. An independent Palestinian state is proposed in an editorial in the *Jordan Times* (Amman), April 8, 1982.

43. An instructive analogy to the problem may be the Anglo-French reaction to the German remilitarization of the Rhineland in 1936.

44. The full text of Husayn's proposal was broadcast on "Radio Amman," March 15, 1972 (reprinted in BBC, *Survey of World Broadcasts*, ME/3942/A6-A11, March 17, 1972). For more on the federal proposal see Zvi El-Peleg, *King Husayn's Federation Plan: Genesis and Reactions*, Shiloah Center Paper 56 (Tel-Aviv, 1979) (Hebrew), and Mark Heller, "Two Variations on the Jordanian Option," in *Is There a Solution to the Palestinian Problem? Israeli Positions*, ed. Alouph Hareven (Jerusalem: Van Leer Foundation, 1982), pp. 99–109 (Hebrew).

4. Security Implications of an Independent Palestinian State

1. These concerns are shared by all the mainstream Zionist parties and are conveniently summarized in a publication of the Israel Information Center, *A Palestinian State: The Case Against* (Jerusalem, 1979). See also Marie Syrkin, "A Palestinian State?" *Midstream* (New York), 20 (October 1974).

2. For a recent reaffirmation of the "strategy of stages" see the interview with Faruq al-Qaddumi, head of the PLO's Political Department, in *Stern* (Hamburg), July 30, 1981, reprinted in *Near East Report*, 25 (October 9, 1981).

3. For hints at a nonbelligerent methodology see interview with al-Qaddumi in *Newsweek*, November 14, 1977, p. 37; interview with Dr. Ahmad Sidqi al-Dajani, member of the PLO Executive Committee, in "Should the Palestinians Change the Charter?" *The Middle East* (London), 63 (January 1980), 23; and interview with Khalid al-Hasan, member of *Fatah's* Central Committee, *al-Ra'i al-'Amm* (Kuwait), April 15, 1980.

4. For example, Bassam al-Shak'a, the deposed mayor of Nablus and unofficial leader of the National Guidance Committee in the occupied territories: "I now want good neighborly relations on the basis of two states—independent Palestine and the State of Israel." *Ha'aretz* (Tel-Aviv), January 6, 1981. See also, interview with the mayors of Hebron and Halhul, Fahd al-Qawasmi and Muhammad Milhim, after their deportation, in *Ruz al-Yusuf* (Cairo), January 12, 1981.

5. See, for example, Sa'id Hammami, PLO representative in London, in *Jerusalem Post*, April 9, 1974. It may be significant that Hammami was assassinated in January 1978, apparently by a dissident Palestinian faction enjoying Iraqi support. *The Middle East* (August 1980), p.18.

6. A vivid description of the sentiments and aspirations of the generation of Palestine is provided in Rosemary Sayigh, *Palestinians: From Peasants to Revolutionaries* (London: Zed Press, 1979), chap. 1. See also Yehoshafat Harkabi, "The Position of the Palestinians in the Arab-Israeli Conflict and the National Covenant (1968)," *New York University Journal of International Law and Politics*, 3 (Spring 1970), 211–214.

7. Yasir 'Arafat's own background is somewhat obscure; his birthplace is variously cited as the Jerusalem region or Gaza. Some other leaders are from outside the Green Line (the late Zuhayr Muhsin, the former head of *Sa'iqa*, was born in Tulkarm) or outside Palestine altogether (Na'if Hawatma, head of the Democratic Front, is a native of Salt in Transjordan). But many of 'Arafat's collaborators or rivals were born in localities now part of Israel: Faruq al-Qaddumi from Jaffa; Salah Khalaf (Abu 'Iyad), head of PLO International Operations and reputed founder of "Black September," also from Jaffa; George Habash, head of the Popular Front for the Liberation of Palestine (PFLP), from Lydda; the late Wadi' Haddad, Habash's former deputy and director of PFLP Special Operations, from Safad; Ahmad Jibril, head of the PFLP—General Command, also from Safad; and Khalid al-Fahum, chairman of the Palestine National Council, from Nazareth. Biographical information drawn from various sources, including Riad el-Rayyes and Dunia Nahas, *Guerrillas for Palestine* (London: Croom Helm, 1976), chap. 6; William B. Quandt, Fuad Jabber, and Ann Mosely Lesch, *The Politics of Palestinian Nationalism* (Berkeley and Los Angeles: University of California Press, 1973), part II; and John Laffin, *Fedayeen: The Arab-Israeli Dilemma* (London: Cassell, 1973), passim.

8. See, for example, Hisham Sharabi, "The Development of PLO Peace Policy," *Middle East International* (London), September 12, 1980, p. 8.

9. For further elaboration on the "erosion and withering away" school of Arab thought see Yehoshafat Harkabi, *Arab Strategies and Israel's Response* (New York: Free Press, 1977), pp. 41–46. A proper evaluation of this potentiality would require a detailed analysis of Israeli social structure and political culture, which is quite beyond the

scope of this study. Suffice it to say that it constitutes a danger for Israelis only insofar as they share Arab perceptions of the nature of the Jewish state.

10. The fears of the rejectionists on this matter are voiced in an interview with Abu 'Ali Mustafa, secretary-general of the PFLP, in *al-Hadaf* (Beirut), December 27, 1980. For a comprehensive overview from the Palestinian perspective see Hussein J. Agha, "What State for the Palestinians?" *Journal of Palestine Studies*, 6 (Autumn 1976), 3–37.

11. Some have argued that before Camp David, West Bankers would have acquiesced in any settlement, including the Jordanian option, that put an end to the Israeli occupation and restored Arab sovereignty. W.F. Abboushi, "Changing Political Attitudes in the West Bank After Camp David," in *A Palestinian Agenda for the West Bank and Gaza*, ed. Emile A. Nakhleh, American Enterprise Institute Study 277 (Washington, 1980), p. 8.

12. Edward W. Said, *The Question of Palestine* (New York: Times Books, 1979), p. 175.

13. Palestinian estimates range from 3 to 4 million, with the lower figure cited by George Kossaifi, "Demographic Characteristics of the Arab Palestinian People," in *The Sociology of the Palestinians*, ed. Khalil Nakhleh and Elia Zureik (London: Croom Helm, 1980), p. 31, and the higher figure recalled by Muhsin D. Yusuf, "The Potential Impact of Palestinian Education on a Palestinian State," *Journal of Palestine Studies*, 8 (Summer 1979), 71. A very high estimate is advanced by the 1980 Statistical Abstract of the Palestine National Fund, as reported in the *Sa'iqa* journal *al-Talai'* (Damascus), December 31, 1980. Israel figures suggest a number slightly lower than 3.5 million. A private Israeli study concluded that total Palestinian population at the end of 1974 was about 2.9 million, which, if extrapolated at 3 percent per annum, would yield a figure of approximately 3.46 million at the end of 1980. See Moshe Efrat, *The Palestinian Refugees: An Economic and Social Research, 1949–1974*, Horowitz Institute Study 10 (Tel-Aviv, 1976), table 26, p. 59 (Hebrew). An official estimate for mid-1980 of Palestinians outside Israel was 2.75 million. Israel, Ministry of Defense, *Fourteen Years of Civil Administration in Judaea and Samaria, Gaza District and Sinai, and the Golan Heights, 1967–1981* (Tel-Aviv, 1982), p. 209 (Hebrew draft). If added to the 639,000 non-Jews in Israel (almost all Arabs), this would bring the total number of Palestinians to 3.39 million.

14. The total refugee population registered with the United Nations Relief and Works Agency in mid-1980 was about 1,844,000, of

whom approximately 688,000 were recorded in refugee camps. These figures refer to both 1948 and 1967 refugees, and the second figure also includes about 8,000 persons not registered as refugees. United Nations, *Report of the Commissioner-General of the United Nations Relief and Works Agency for Palestine Refugees in the Near East, 1 July 1979–30 June 1980*, tables 1 and 4, pp. 58 and 64 (hereafter cited as *UNRWA Report*). Because of false or duplicate registrations and unreported deaths or absences, and because of the refusal of Arab host governments to permit a proper census, these figures are undoubtedly inflated, and UNRWA itself "presumes that the refugee population present in the area of UNRWA operations is less than the registered population." Ibid., table 1, p. 59. Nevertheless, unless otherwise specified, UNRWA figures will be used in this analysis because they provide the only series consistent over time. According to Israeli data, 21 percent of the Palestinian population in the West Bank and Gaza (refugees and nonrefugees together) are aged thirty-five or over. Computed from Israel, Central Bureau of Statistics, *Statistical Abstract of Israel*, no. 32 (1981), table xxvii/3, p. 714 (hereafter cited as *Statistical Abstract*). If this age structure is applied to the total refugee population, the generation of Palestine appears to consist of approximately 387,000 souls, about 11 percent of all Palestinians. Of the camp population, only about 144,500 would be thirty-five or over, approximately 4 percent of the total.

15. The phrase *maku awamir* (there are no orders), used by Iraqi units of the Arab League-controlled Arab Liberation Army to justify their passivity in 1948, is recalled with particular rancor. Sayigh, *Palestinians*, p. 79.

16. Skepticism about the commitment of Arab states in the current stage is expressed by three former West Bank mayors, Shak'a, Qawasmi, and Milhim, in "The Mood of the West Bank," *Journal of Palestine Studies*, 9 (Autumn 1979), 115–116. Former mayor Karim Khalaf of Ramallah has claimed that "80 percent of the Arab states" oppose a Palestinian state lest it endanger their own regimes. *Al-Hadaf*, August 30, 1980, p. 11.

17. Walid Khalidi, "Thinking the Unthinkable: A Sovereign Palestinian State," *Foreign Affairs*, 56 (July 1978), 698–699.

18. This endorsement was the seventh point of an eight-point plan revealed by Saudi Crown Prince Fahd in an interview on "Radio Riyadh" on August 7, 1981 (text in BBC, *Survey of World Broadcasts*, ME/6797/A/1, August 10, 1981).

19. See, for example, *Ma'ariv* (Tel-Aviv), September 22, 1981; *In-*

ternational Herald Tribune, October 18, 1981; *Jerusalem Post*, January 8, 1982.

20. For an elaboration on this possibility see Zvi Lanir, *The Israeli Involvement in Lebanon — Precedent for an "Open" Game with Syria?* Center for Strategic Studies Paper 10 (Tel Aviv, 1980).

21. See Yehezkel Dror, *Crazy States: A Counterconventional Strategic Problem* (Lexington, Mass.: D.C. Heath, 1971).

22. Ibid., p. 38.

23. Ibid., p. 97.

24. Emile A. Nakhleh, "Reflections on the Agenda," in Nakhleh, ed., *A Palestinian Agenda*, p. 4. See also, Hisham Sharabi, "Creating Palestine," *New York Times*, December 20, 1981.

25. Personal interview with Muhammad Hallaj, Dean of the Faculty of Arts, Bir Zeit University, November 11, 1980.

26. Muhammad Hallaj, "Mission of Palestinian Higher Education," in Nakhleh, ed., *A Palestinian Agenda*, p. 73.

27. Personal interview with Zafir al-Masri, deputy mayor of Nablus and chairman of the Chamber of Commerce, January 1, 1981.

28. The census conducted by Israel in the summer of 1967 revealed that 96.7 percent of the population of the West Bank and Gaza were Muslims. Israel, Central Bureau of Statistics and Israel Defense Forces, *Census of Population, 1967, Publication No. 1: Data from Full Enumeration* (Jerusalem, 1967), p. 12. Even if East Jerusalem, with its greater concentration of Christians, were included, Muslims would still constitute 95.3 percent of the population. On East Jerusalem population see Israel, Central Bureau of Statistics and Municipality of Jerusalem, *Census of Population and Housing, 1967: East Jerusalem*, part I (Jerusalem, 1968), table I. In recent years, the Christian element has apparently grown even smaller; a disproportionate number of emigrants have come from the Christian communities.

29. According to one survey, Palestinians by the late 1960s had already acquired university education in about the same numbers as Israelis; among university graduates, about 17 percent were working in engineering positions and another 15 percent in management. Nabeel Sha'ath, "High Level Palestinian Manpower," *Journal of Palestine Studies*, 1 (Winter 1972), 91–94; also Yusuf, "The Potential Impact of Palestinian Education."

30. For more on this theme see Bernard Lewis, "The Return of Islam," *Commentary*, 61 (January 1976), 42.

31. At the beginning of 1980, students in the Islamic College of

Gaza, which is affiliated with al-Azhar University in Cairo, torched the offices of the leftist-dominated Palestine Red Crescent Society and then attacked other symbols of "apostasy," such as cinemas and restaurants serving alcohol. *Jerusalem Post*, January 11, 1980.

32. For more on the position of Christians during the Mandate period see Daphne Tsimhoni, "The Arab Christians and the Palestinian National Movement During the Formative Stage," in *The Palestinians and the Middle East Conflict: Studies in Their History, Sociology and Politics*, ed. Gabriel Ben-Dor (Ramat-Gan: Turtledove, 1979), pp. 73–98.

33. On the religious world view of the Palestinian intelligentsia in the early 1970s see Shimon Shamir and others, *The Professional Elite in Samaria* (Tel-Aviv: Shiloah Center, 1975), pp. 23–26 (Hebrew).

34. This trend is discussed in greater detail in Mark Heller, "Politics and Social Change in the West Bank Since 1967," in *Palestinian Society and Politics*, ed. Joel S. Migdal (Princeton: Princeton University Press, 1980), pp. 187–195.

35. Sayigh, *Palestinians*, p. 178.

36. Ibid., p. 185, n. 24.

37. For one example of the suspicion that a Palestine-state solution would facilitate domination by the Palestinian right see the interview with Abu 'Ali Mustafa, *al-Hadaf*, December 27, 1980.

38. For example, Salah Khalaf [Abu 'Iyad], interview with Eric Rouleau, cited in *Jerusalem Post International Edition*, January 14–20, p. 10.

39. This assumption is shared by Yusuf, "The Potential Impact of Palestinian Education," p. 92.

40. See Agha, "What State for the Palestinians?" pp. 22–23.

41. Explicitly class-oriented, hence divisive, politics may well flourish in the more congenial circumstances of independence. The Communist party is already a small but highly disciplined and cohesive organization. See, for example, Amnon Kapeliuk, "Communism in the West Bank," *New Outlook* (Tel-Aviv), 23 (May 1980), 18–21.

42. *Al-Anba* (Jerusalem), September 2, 1977, cited in *Middle East Contemporary Survey*, vol. I: 1976–77, p. 215.

43. For an overview of West Bank criticisms of the PLO that tends, if anything, toward understatement see Michael C. Hudson, "The Scars of Occupation: An Eye-Witness Report," *Journal of Palestine Studies*, 9 (Winter 1980), 42–44. Some residents of the West Bank reportedly felt that the new PLO Executive Committee elected at the fifteenth session of the Palestine National Council did not adequately

represent those bearing the main burden of the Israeli occupation. *Ha'aretz*, April 21, 1981.

44. On the marginality of the 1948 refugees in West Bank society and politics see Avi Plascov, *The Palestinian Refugees in Jordan, 1948–1957* (London: Frank Cass, 1981), especially chap. 6.

45. The structural basis for these subregional loyalties (economic, educational, and so forth) was elaborated in a personal interview with Anan Safadi, Arab affairs correspondent of the *Jerusalem Post*, on January 28, 1974, and subsequently corroborated in many personal discussions with West Bank personalities.

46. My computation from *Statistical Abstract*, no. 32 (1981), table xxvii/6, pp. 716–717.

47. For figures on Israeli and local personnel in governmental health, welfare, and educational services in the West Bank and Gaza see Israel, Ministry of Defense, Coordinator of Government Operations in Judea–Samaria, Gaza District, Sinai, *A Fourteen Year Survey (1967–1981)* (Tel-Aviv, 1982), Appendix 21, p. 55. The activities of UNRWA and the voluntary societies are described in Emile A. Nakhleh, *The West Bank and Gaza: Toward the Making of a Palestinian State*, American Enterprise Institute Study 232 (Washington, 1979), chap. 3.

48. The quasi-governmental structure of the PLO is described in Rashid Hamid, "What Is the PLO?" *Journal of Palestine Studies*, 4 (Summer 1975), 90–109. *Samed*, a welfare institution founded to provide for Palestinian widows and orphans in the wake of the Lebanese civil war, developed into an extensive industrial conglomerate involved in manufacturing, vehicle maintenance, agricultural research, printing and film production, and public health. Its activities are described in "Details on the *Samed* Institution," *Samed al-Iqtisadi* (Beirut), January 12, 1980.

49. Another forecast of modest economic expectations is given in Elias H. Tuma, "The Economic Viability of a Palestine State," *Journal of Palestine Studies*, 7 (Spring 1978), 103–104.

50. Average annual growth rate for the period 1976–1980, computed from data in *Statistical Abstract*, no. 32 (1981), table xxvii/1, p. 713.

51. In 1977, East Bank GNP per capita was $870 and growing at an annual rate of about 10 percent. United States, Central Intelligence Agency, *National Basic Intelligence Factbook* (1980), p. 103. In the same year, GNP per capita in the occupied territories was about $775 (higher in the West Bank, lower in Gaza), and growing at about 5 per-

cent per year. *Statistical Abstract*, no. 32 (1981), table xxvii/6, pp. 716–717. The 1977 dollar figure for the West Bank and Gaza is based on an exchange rate of $ = I£ (Israeli pounds) 11.12, computed from data in table ix/11, p. 238.

52. Regarding numbers of expected immigrants, the low figure is assumed by Hisham M. Awartani, "Agriculture," in Nakhleh, ed., *A Palestinian Agenda*, p. 15, and by Bethlehem mayor Ilyas Freij, "Is-raeli-Palestinian Dialogue," *Migvan* (Tel-Aviv), nos. 50–51 (August-September 1980), 5 (Hebrew); the higher figure is given in Elias H. Tuma and Haim Darin-Drabkin, *Palestinian Independence — The Economic Aspect* (Tel-Aviv, 1979), p. 60 (Hebrew). Awartani assumes that the migration would be effected within one year; Freij asserts that it could take place "within a period of 10–15 years."

53. Figure cited in Efrat, *The Palestinian Refugees*, Appendix B-5.

54. Kossaifi, "Demographic Characteristics," pp. 28–29; Sayigh, *Palestinians*, p. 111; A. Khalidi and H. Agha, "The Palestinian Diaspora," *The Middle East Yearbook 1980* (London), p. 32.

55. *UNRWA Report*, table 4, p. 64.

56. Ibid.

57. A transition period of similar length is assumed in Tuma, "The Economic Viability," p. 118.

58. The average growth rate for the entire refugee population dur-ing the period 1975–1980, computed from *UNRWA Report*, table 1, p. 58.

59. Labor force participation rate computed from *Statistical Abstract*, no. 32 (1981), tables xxvii/1, p. 713, and xxvii/17, pp. 728–729.

60. For an attempt to treat some of these issues in greater detail see Nakhleh, ed., *A Palestinian Agenda*.

61. The potential magnitude of the problem is illustrated by the case of the town of Jenin, in northern Samaria, which transacts about 60 percent of its commerce with Israeli residents. Fredy Zack, "The Development of Jenin in the Years 1967–1975," in *Judea and Samaria: Studies in Settlement Geography*, vol. II, ed. Avshalom Shmueli, David Grussman, and Rehavam Ze'evi (Jerusalem: Canaan Publish-ing, 1977), p. 257 (Hebrew).

62. *Statistical Abstract*, no. 32 (1981), table xxvii/19, p. 732.

63. Efrat, *The Palestinian Refugees*, table C-6. Estimates vary.

64. Imputed from yearly population figures in *Statistical Abstract*, no. 32 (1981), table xxvii/1, p. 713.

65. West Bank figure from Israel, Central Bureau of Statistics, *Ad-*

ministered Territories Statistics Quarterly, 10 (December 1980), 95 (hereafter cited as *ATSQ*); Gaza figure from Tuma and Darin-Drabkin, *Palestinian Independence*, p. 83. One dunam = ¼ acre.

66. Water resources in the West Bank and Gaza are discussed in detail in *A Fourteen Year Survey*, pp. 11–15. In 1979–80, the water balance between Israel and the West Bank was actually 1,069,000 million cubic meters in favor of the latter. Ibid., p. 11. On potential water resources see "Israel and the Resources of the West Bank," *Journal of Palestine Studies*, 8 (Summer 1979), 97–99.

67. In 1973–74, land under cultivation totaled 1,758,000 dunams. *ATSQ*, 5 (1975), 79–80.

68. Tuma and Darin-Drabkin, *Palestinian Independence*, p. 82.

69. It has been estimated that 200 million cubic meters, an infinitesimal fraction of the Nile's annual flow, could eliminate the existing shortfall in Gaza and provide enough to water all the irrigable land in the Strip. Ephraim Ahiram, "Open-eyed in Gaza," *Jerusalem Post*, December 2, 1981.

70. Yusuf, "The Potential Impact of Palestinian Education," p. 92.

71. *UNRWA Report*, table 13, pp. 73–74; *A Fourteen Year Survey*, Appendix 28, p. 67.

72. Ghassan Harb, "Labor and Manpower," in Nakhleh, ed., *A Palestinian Agenda*, p. 100.

73. See Raphael Meron, *The Economy of the Administered Territories, 1977–1978* (Jerusalem: Bank of Israel Research Department, 1980), pp. 9–10 (Hebrew); Brian Van Arkadie, *Benefits and Burdens: A Report on the West Bank and Gaza Strip Economies Since 1967* (New York and Washington: Carnegie Endowment for International Peace, 1977), pp. 106-110. Information in this section computed from data in *ATSQ*, 11 (February 1982), Appendix 1, "National Accounts of Judaea and Samaria, the Gaza Strip and North Sinai," pp. 63–74.

74. *UNRWA Report*, table C, p. 48 (for budget figure) and table 4, p. 64 (for population figure).

75. Baghdad Conference pledge cited in *al-Anwar* (Beirut), November 10, 1978; gross revenue figure reported in *Jerusalem Post*, October 24, 1979 (citing the *Wall Street Journal*).

76. United States, Library of Congress, Congressional Research Service, *West Bank and Gaza Economy: Problems and Prospects*, report prepared for US, House of Representatives, Committee on Foreign Affairs, Subcommittee on Europe and the Middle East, reprinted in *Leviathan* (Boston), 3 (Fall 1980), 45. This analysis assumes no significant immigration during the transition period.

77. *Statistical Abstract*, no. 32 (1981), tables xxvii/4, p. 724, and xxvii/15, p. 725.

78. See Chapter 4.

79. See Fouad Ajami, "The End of Pan-Arabism," *Foreign Affairs*, 57 (Winter 1978–79), 365–369.

80. Galia Golan, *Soviet-PLO Relations and the Creation of a Palestinian State*, Soviet and East European Research Center Paper 36 (Jerusalem, 1979), pp. 5–7.

81. For more on the Communist party and the PNF see Amnon Cohen, "The Changing Pattern of West Bank Politics," *The Jerusalem Quarterly*, no. 5 (Fall 1977), 106–110.

82. See, for example, "The Palestinian Problem and a Middle East Settlement," *Mezhdunarodnaia Zhizn* (Moscow), no. 6 (1980).

83. The three PNF representatives elected to the Executive Committee in 1977 were 'Abd al-Muhsin Abu Mayzir, Walid Qamhawi, and 'Abd al-Jawwad Salih. *Arab Report and Record* (London), no. 6, April 29, 1977, p. 277. All had been deported from the West Bank in December 1973. A fourth electee, Alfred Tubasi of Ramallah, was officially listed as an independent, although he, too, was reported to have been a leader of the PNF at the time of his deportation in November 1974. *Yedi'ot Aharonot* (Tel-Aviv), November 22, 1974. Because of its inability to agree on a new formula for representation, the fourteenth PNC in 1979 left the existing Executive Committee intact; in 1981, new elections were held, and of the four incumbents, only Abu Mayzir retained his seat. "Radio Damascus," April 19, 1981 (cited in BBC, *Survey of World Broadcasts*, ME/6703/A/5, April 21, 1981).

5. Potential Implications for Other Israeli Interests

1. Israel, Central Bureau of Statistics, *Statistical Abstract of Israel*, no. 32 (1981), table ii/1, p. 30 (hereafter cited as *Statistical Abstract*).

2. In 1980, the non-Jewish rate of natural increase was 3.3 percent per annum; the Jewish rate was only 1.5 percent. Computed from ibid., table ii/2, p. 31.

3. See, for example, Mark A. Tessler, "Israel's Arabs and the Palestinian Problem," *Middle East Journal*, 31 (Summer 1977); John E. Hofman and Benjamin Beit-Hallahmi, "The Palestinian Identity and Israel's Arabs," in *The Palestinians and the Middle East Conflict: Studies in Their History, Sociology and Politics*, ed. Gabriel Ben-Dor

(Ramat-Gan: Turtledove, 1979); Elie Rekhess, "Israeli Arab Intelligentsia," *The Jerusalem Quarterly*, no. 11 (Spring 1979); and Ian Lustick, "The Quiescent Palestinians: The System of Control over Arabs in Israel," in *The Sociology of the Palestinians*, ed. Khalil Nakhleh and Elia Zureik (London: Croom Helm, 1980).

4. Rekhess, "Israeli Arab Intelligentsia," pp. 54–57. But Tessler reports the interesting finding that Arab secondary school graduates are more likely to identify with Israel than those with either primary only or university education. "Israel's Arabs," p. 322.

5. Ibid., pp. 327–328. Also, Hanan Rapaport, director of the Henrietta Szold Institute for the Behavioral Sciences, interview in the *Jerusalem Post*, November 9, 1979; and Atallah Mansur, a prominent Israeli Arab journalist, interviews in *Newsweek*, April 12, 1976, and *Los Angeles Times*, April 12, 1981.

6. See interviews with Tawfiq Zayyad, mayor of Nazareth, *New York Times*, August 25, 1980, and Emile Touma, editor-in-chief of the Rakah newspaper *al-Ittihad*, in *Leviathan* (Boston), 3 (Fall 1980), 40–44. See also the assertion in the Knesset of Rakah M. K. Tawfiq Toubi that the PLO does not represent Israeli Arabs. *Ma'ariv* (Tel-Aviv), December 4, 1980.

7. For example, Lustick, "The Quiescent Palestinians," p. 80.

8. 29 percent claimed both identities; 7 percent chose neither. Tessler, "Israel's Arabs," pp. 316–317.

9. Cited in Rekhess, "Israeli Arab Intelligentsia," p. 64. The "Triangle" (or "Little Triangle") is an area inside pre-1967 Israel densely populated by Arabs. It is directly opposite the "Big Triangle" of Jenin–Tulkarm–Nablus in the West Bank.

10. Atallah Mansur, "Rakah's Rivals," *Ha'aretz* (Tel-Aviv), December 1, 1980.

11. Tessler, "Israel's Arabs," p. 325.

12. Rekhess, "Israeli Arab Intelligentsia," p. 54.

13. Statement by Prime Minister Begin, *Jerusalem Post*, March 1, 1981. A map published in March 1981 by the Jewish Agency Settlement Department and the World Zionist Organization Settlement Division showed eighty settlements. These figures exclude settlements within the expanded municipal boundaries of Jerusalem. There were also nine settlements built or under construction in the Gaza Strip. Ten months later, the number of settlers had reached 23,000. *Jerusalem Post*, January 31, 1982. According to Defense Minister Ariel Sharon, there were to have been 30,000 Jewish settlers in 102 "settlement points" by the summer of 1982. Cited on "Israel Defense Forces

Radio," April 5, 1982 (text of report printed in BBC, *Survey of World Broadcasts*, ME/6998/A/4, April 7, 1982).

14. *Jerusalem Post*, November 11, 1980. More settlements had been planned.

15. Information from Israel Government Press Office, November 13, 1980.

16. *Jerusalem Post*, April 6, 1981.

17. Jewish Agency/World Zionist Organization, *Settlement Map of the Land of Israel* (Jerusalem, 1981).

18. *Jerusalem Post*, March 19, 1982. My emphasis.

19. See the judgment of Supreme Court Justice Moshe Landau in "Law Report," *Jerusalem Post*, November 1, 1979.

20. Moshe Dayan, quoted in the *New York Times*, January 31, 1973. For more on the military role of the settlements see Aryeh Shalev, *The West Bank: Line of Defense* (Tel-Aviv: Hakibbutz Hameuhad, 1982) (Hebrew).

21. Zvi Shuldiner, "The Real Cost of the Settlements," *Ha'aretz*, July 25, 1980; David Richardson, "New Samaria Settlements Being Dedicated Before Vote," *Jerusalem Post*, June 25, 1981.

22. See the interview with Ra'anan Weitz, head of the World Zionist Organization Settlement Department, *Jerusalem Post International Edition*, September 20, 1977.

23. United States, Library of Congress, Congressional Research Service, *West Bank and Gaza Economy: Problems and Prospects*, report prepared for U.S., House of Representatives, Committee on Foreign Affairs, Subcommittee on Europe and the Middle East, reprinted in *Leviathan*, 3 (Fall 1980), 48.

24. A poll carried out in the spring of 1981 showed that over 60 percent of a representative sample were in favor of continuing settlement in Judaea and Samaria, including over 30 percent who supported settlement everywhere and without any restrictions or conditions. *Jerusalem Post*, March 31,1981.

25. Saul B. Cohen, *Jerusalem, Bridging the Four Walls: A Geopolitical Perspective* (New York: Herzl Press, 1977), p. 46.

26. See, for example, Teddy Kollek, "Jerusalem," *Foreign Affairs*, 55 (July 1977), 703.

27. At the end of 1980, the non-Jewish population within the municipal boundaries of Jerusalem was 114,800. Computed from *Statistical Abstract*, no. 32 (1981), table ii/13, p. 46.

28. Walid Khalidi, "Thinking the Unthinkable: A Sovereign Palestinian State," *Foreign Affairs*, 56, (July 1978), 705.

29. For some of the best examples of imaginative thinking within the Israeli paradigm see Kollek, "Jerusalem," and interview in the *Jerusalem Post Magazine*, February 1, 1980; Cohen, *Jerusalem*, pp. 115–123; and Meron Benvenisti, "An Eternal Problem," *Jerusalem Post Magazine*, February 8, 1980, and "Status and Sovereignty," *Jerusalem Post Magazine*, February 22,1980.

30. By the end of 1979, over 55,000 Jews were living in those parts of Jerusalem under Jordanian control before 1967. Michael Romann, "Jews and Arabs in Jerusalem," *The Jerusalem Quarterly*, no. 19 (Spring 1981), 39.

31. See, for example, Khalidi, "Thinking the Unthinkable," and Anwar Nusaybah, *Jerusalem Post*, May 29, 1980.

32. *Statistical Abstract*, no. 32 (1981), table xxvii/11, p. 721.

33. Ibid., table vii/2, p. 192.

34. Calculated from figures for Israeli and West Bank/Gaza GNP, ibid., tables vi/2, p. 164, and xxvii/6, pp. 716–717.

35. See Ephraim Ahiram, "Economics and a Palestinian State," *Jerusalem Post*, October 5, 1981.

36. Computed from *Statistical Abstract*, no. 32 (1981), table vi/10, p. 179.

37. Ibid., table xii/1, pp. 318–319.

38. Ibid., tables xii/12, pp. 336–337, and xxvii/19, p. 732.

39. The oft-expressed fear that workers from the territories would become a politically volatile "reserve army of the unemployed" has not been borne out by experience. Contrary to expectations, economic slowdowns have produced unemployment in Israel itself without affecting full employment in the territories, apparently because workers from the West Bank and Gaza are prepared to do jobs for which Israeli workers consider themselves overqualified. A similar phenomenon has been observed with respect to migrant or illegal workers in Western Europe and North America. In 1980, 63,600 Israelis were unemployed, even while 71,900 West Bank/Gaza residents continued to work in Israel. Ibid., table xii/1, pp. 332–333.

40. About two-thirds of the building stone used in the Jerusalem area is supplied by Bethlehem or Hebron quarries. Discussion with Captain Ishai Cohen, Economic Staff Officer, Judaea and Samaria Area Command, June 9, 1981.

41. Aryeh Shalev, *The Autonomy—Problems and Possible Solutions*, Center for Strategic Studies Paper 8 (Tel-Aviv, 1980), p. 138.

42. Ibid. See also "Israel and the Resources of the West Bank," *Journal of Palestine Studies*, 8 (Summer 1979), 97.

43. US, Library of Congress, *West Bank and Gaza Economy*, p. 48.

44. Ibid., p. 50.

6. Israeli Requirements for Risk Minimization

1. For more on a neutral Palestinian state and various attitudes toward it see John Edwin Mroz, *Beyond Security: Private Perceptions Among Arabs and Israelis* (New York: International Peace Academy, 1980), pp. 138–163.

2. See, for example, the acknowledgment that Israel needs early warning stations by Naffez Nazzal, "Land Tenure, the Settlements and Peace," in *A Palestinian Agenda for the West Bank and Gaza*, ed. Emile A. Nakhleh, American Enterprise Institute Study 277 (Washington, 1980), p. 118.

3. Walid Khalidi, "Thinking the Unthinkable: A Sovereign Palestinian State," *Foreign Affairs*, 56 (July 1978), 703. See also Valerie Yorke, "Palestinian Self-Determination and Israel's Security," *Journal of Palestine Studies*, 8 (Spring 1979), 16–17.

4. The primary determinant of the permissible size of the Palestinian army would be Israeli security considerations, but the fact that the Palestine Liberation Army also consists of three brigades means that most of its members could be absorbed into the new Palestinian army (with some changes in the upper command), thus avoiding the political danger of unemployed and potentially disgruntled officers and soldiers. Several thousands of former *fida'iyyun* would have to be provided for in some other way.

5. Yorke, "Palestinian Self-Determination, p. 18. The PLO has not specifically addressed the issue of arms limitations, except for some fleeting references by Yasir 'Arafat to a possible role for international observer forces along the frontiers. Interview with Anthony Lewis, *New York Times*, May 2, 1978. Nevertheless, the fact that arms limitations proposals were published in the *Journal of Palestine Studies*, an organ of the Institute for Palestine Studies in Beirut, suggests that the basic idea is not excluded.

6. Based on Israel, Israel Defense Forces, Spokesman, *PLO Terror—A Statistical Summary* (Tel-Aviv, 1981). Figures exclude the period October 7–26, 1973.

7. This appears to be one of the principal Palestinian objections to the Camp David autonomy agreement. See Mark Heller, "Begin's

False Autonomy," *Foreign Policy*, no. 37 (Winter 1979–80), 116–117.

7. The Calculus of Decision

1. For a further elaboration of the case for public acceptance by Israel of a Palestinian state see Yehoshafat Harkabi, *Arab Strategies and Israel's Response* (New York: Free Press, 1977), pp. 147–149.

Bibliography

Newspapers and Periodicals Consulted

al-Anba' (Jerusalem)
al-Anwar (Beirut)
Arab Report and Record (London)
Ha'aretz (Tel-Aviv)
al-Hadaf (Beirut)
ila l'Amam (Beirut)
International Herald Tribune (Paris)
Jerusalem Post
Jerusalem Post International Edition
Jordan Times (Amman)
al-Liwa' (Beirut)
Los Angeles Times
Ma'ariv (Tel-Aviv)
al-Majalla (London)
Monday Morning (Beirut)
al-Nahar al-'Arabi wa'l Dawli (Paris)
New York Times
al-Ra'i al-'Amm (Kuwait)
Ruz al-Yusuf (Cairo)
The Sunday Times (London)
al-Talai' (Damascus)
United Kingdom, British Broadcasting Corporation, *Survey of World Broadcasts*
United States, Foreign Broadcast Information Service, *Daily Report*
Yedi'ot Aharonot (Tel-Aviv)

Books and Articles

Agha, Hussein J. "What State for the Palestinians?" *Journal of Palestine Studies*, 6 (Autumn 1976).

Ajami, Fouad. "The End of Pan-Arabism," *Foreign Affairs*, 57 (Winter 1978–79).

Allon, Yigal. "Israel: The Case for Defensible Borders," *Foreign Affairs*, 55 (October 1976).

_____ "The West Bank and Gaza Within the Framework of a Middle East Peace Settlement," *Middle East Review*, 12 (Winter 1979–80).

Ben-Dor, Gabriel, ed. *The Palestinians and the Middle East Conflict: Studies in Their History, Sociology and Politics.* Ramat-Gan: Turtledove, 1979.

Ben-Zvi, Abraham. *The Reagan Presidency and the Palestinian Predicament: An Interim Analysis.* Center for Strategic Studies Paper 16. Tel-Aviv, 1982.

_____ *The United States and the Palestinians: The Carter Era.* Center for Strategic Studies Paper 13. Tel-Aviv, 1981.

Cohen, Amnon. "The Changing Pattern of West Bank Politics," *The Jerusalem Quarterly*, no. 5 (Fall 1977).

Cohen, Saul B. *Jerusalem, Bridging the Four Walls: A Geopolitical Perspective.* New York: Herzl Press, 1977.

Dror, Yehezkel. *Crazy States: A Counterconventional Strategic Problem.* Lexington, Mass.: D. C. Heath, 1971.

Efrat, Moshe. *The Palestinian Refugees: An Economic and Social Research, 1949–1974.* David Horowitz Institute for Research on Developing Countries, Study 10. Tel-Aviv, 1976 (Hebrew).

Elazar, Daniel J. *Arrangements for Self-Rule and Autonomy in Various Countries of the World: A Preliminary Inventory.* Jerusalem: Jerusalem Institute for Federal Studies, 1978.

_____ *The Camp David Framework for Peace: A Shift Toward Shared Rule.* American Enterprise Institute for Public Policy Research, Study 236. Washington, 1979.

_____ and Ira Sharkansky. *Alternative Federal Solutions to the Problem of the Administered Territories.* Jerusalem: Jerusalem Institute for Federal Studies, 1978.

_____ and others. *Israel, the Palestinians, and the Territories: Some Alternative Frameworks for Peace.* Jerusalem: Jerusalem Institute for Federal Studies, 1981.

El-Peleg, Zvi. *King Husayn's Federation Plan: Genesis and Reactions.* Shiloah Center for Middle Eastern and African Studies Paper 56. Tel-Aviv, 1979 (Hebrew).

Gilbert, Martin. *The Arab-Israeli Conflict: Its History in Maps.* London: Weidenfeld and Nicholson, 1974.

Golan, Galia. *Soviet-PLO Relations and the Creation of a Palestinian State.* Soviet and East European Research Center Paper 36. Jerusalem, 1979.

Hamid, Rashid. "What Is the PLO?" *Journal of Palestine Studies,* 4 (Summer 1975).

Harkabi, Yehoshafat. *Arab Strategies and Israel's Response.* New York: Free Press, 1977.

_____ "The Palestinians in the Fifties and Their Awakening as Reflected in Their Literature," in *Palestinian Arab Politics,* ed. Moshe Maoz. Jerusalem: Jerusalem Academic Press, 1975.

_____ "The Position of the Palestinians in the Arab-Israeli Conflict and the National Covenant (1968)," *New York University Journal of International Law and Politics,* 3 (Spring 1970).

Hartman, Moshe. *Jewish and Arab Population in Eretz Yisrael: The Year 2000.* Tel-Aviv: Tel-Aviv University Project on Criteria for Defining Secure Borders, n.d. (Hebrew).

Heller, Mark A. "Begin's False Autonomy," *Foreign Policy,* no. 37 (Winter 1979–80).

_____ "Politics and Social Change in the West Bank Since 1967," in *Palestinian Society and Politics,* ed. Joel S. Migdal. Princeton: Princeton University Press, 1980.

_____ "Two Variations on the Jordanian Option," in *Is There a Solution to the Palestinian Problem? Israeli Positions,* ed. Alouph Hareven. Jerusalem: Van Leer Foundation, 1982 (Hebrew).

_____ "Voices from the West Bank," *Moment* (Boston), 3 (April 1978).

_____ "The Vulnerability of the Third Force," *Leviathan* (Boston), 2 (Spring 1978).

_____, ed. *The Middle East Military Balance.* Tel-Aviv: Center for Strategic Studies, forthcoming.

Hudson, Michael C. "The Scars of Occupation: An Eye-Witness Report," *Journal of Palestine Studies,* 9 (Winter 1980).

Israel. Central Bureau of Statistics. *Administered Territories Statistics Quarterly.*

_____ _____ *Statistical Abstract of Israel.* Annual.

_____ _____ and Israel Defense Forces. *Census of Population, 1967. Publication No. 1: Data from Full Enumeration.* Jerusalem, 1967.

_____ _____ and Municipality of Jerusalem. *Census of Population and Housing, 1967: East Jerusalem.* Part I. Jerusalem, 1968.

_____ Israel Information Center. *A Palestinian State: The Case Against.* Jerusalem, 1979.

_____ Israel Defense Forces. Spokesman. *PLO Terror — A Statistical Summary.* Tel-Aviv, 30 March 1981.

_____ Ministry of Defense. *Fourteen Years of Civil Administration in Judaea and Samaria, Gaza District and Sinai, and the Golan Heights, 1967-1981.* Tel-Aviv, 1982 (Hebrew draft).

_____ _____ Coordinator of Government Operations in Judea-Samaria, Gaza District, Sinai. *A Fourteen Year Survey (1967-1981).* Tel-Aviv, 1982.

_____ Ministry for Foreign Affairs. Center for Research and Political Planning. *Documents.*

"Israel and the Resources of the West Bank," *Journal of Palestine Studies,* 8 (Summer 1979).

Israel Labor Party. *Resolutions of the Third Party Conference.* Tel-Aviv, 1981 (Hebrew).

Jewish Agency/World Zionist Organization. *Settlement Map of the Land of Israel.* Jerusalem, March 1981.

Kapeliuk, Amnon. "Communism in the West Bank," *New Outlook* (Tel-Aviv), 23 (May 1980).

Khalidi, A., and H. Agha. "The Palestinian Diaspora," in *The Middle East Yearbook 1980.* London, n.d.

Khalidi, Walid. "Thinking the Unthinkable: A Sovereign Palestinian State," *Foreign Affairs,* 56 (July 1978).

Kollek, Teddy. "Jerusalem," *Foreign Affairs,* 55 (July 1977).

Laffin, John. *Fedayeen: The Arab-Israeli Dilemma.* London: Cassell, 1973.

Lanir, Zvi. *The Israeli Involvement in Lebanon — Precedent for an "Open" Game with Syria?* Center for Strategic Studies Paper 10. Tel-Aviv, 1980.

Legum, Colin, ed. *Middle East Contemporary Survey.* New York and London: Holmes and Meier, annual.

Lewis, Bernard. "The Return of Islam," *Commentary,* 61 (January 1976).

Litani, Yehuda. "Leadership in the West Bank and Gaza," *The Jerusalem Quarterly,* no. 14 (Winter 1980).

Meron, Raphael. *The Economy of the Administered Territories, 1977-1978.* Jerusalem: Bank of Israel Research Department, 1980 (Hebrew).

"The Mood of the West Bank," *Journal of Palestine Studies,* 9 (Autumn 1979).

Moore, John Norton, ed. *The Arab-Israeli Conflict*, vol. III, *Documents*. Princeton: Princeton University Press, 1974.

Mroz, John Edwin. *Beyond Security: Private Perceptions Among Arabs and Israelis*. New York: International Peace Academy, 1980.

Nakhleh, Emile A. *The West Bank and Gaza: Toward the Making of a Palestinian State*. American Enterprise Institute for Public Policy Research Study 232. Washington, 1979.

_____, ed. *A Palestinian Agenda for the West Bank and Gaza*. American Enterprise Institute for Public Policy Research Study 277. Washington, 1980.

Nakhleh, Khalil, and Elia Zureik, eds. *The Sociology of the Palestinians*. London: Croom Helm, 1980.

Plascov, Avi. "The 'Palestinian Gap' Between Israel and Egypt," *Survival*, 22 (March–April 1980).

_____ *The Palestinian Refugees in Jordan, 1948–1957*. London: Frank Cass, 1981.

Quandt, William B., Fuad Jabber, and Ann Mosely Lesch. *The Politics of Palestinian Nationalism*. Berkeley and Los Angeles: University of California Press, 1973.

Raviv, Yehoshua. *The Arab-Israeli Military Balance*. Center for Strategic Studies Paper 7. Tel-Aviv, 1980.

el-Rayyes, Riad, and Dunia Nahas. *Guerrillas for Palestine*. London: Croom Helm, 1976.

Rekhess, Elie. "Israeli Arab Intelligentsia," *The Jerusalem Quarterly*, no. 11 (Spring 1979).

Romann, Michael. "Jews and Arabs in Jerusalem," *The Jerusalem Quarterly*, no. 19 (Spring 1981).

Safran, Nadav. *Israel: The Embattled Ally*. Cambridge, Mass.: Harvard University Press, 1978.

Said, Edward W. *The Question of Palestine*. New York: Times Books, 1979.

Sayigh, Rosemary. *Palestinians: From Peasants to Revolutionaries*. London: Zed Press, 1979.

Schelling, Thomas C. *The Strategy of Conflict*. Oxford: Oxford University Press, 1960.

Sha'ath, Nabeel. "High Level Palestinian Manpower," *Journal of Palestine Studies*, 1 (Winter 1972).

Shalev, Aryeh. *The Autonomy — Problems and Possible Solutions*. Center for Strategic Studies Paper 8. Tel-Aviv, 1980.

_____ *The West Bank: Line of Defense*. Tel-Aviv: Hakibbutz

Hameuhad, 1982 (Hebrew).

Shamir, Shimon, and others. *The Professional Elite in Samaria.* Tel-Aviv: Shiloah Center for Middle Eastern and African Studies, 1975 (Hebrew).

Sharabi, Hisham. "The Development of PLO Peace Policy," *Middle East International* (London), September 12, 1980.

Syrkin, Marie. "A Palestinian State?" *Midstream* (New York), 20 (October 1974).

Tessler, Mark A. "Israel's Arabs and the Palestinian Problem," *Middle East Journal,* 31 (Summer 1977).

Tuma, Elias H. "The Economic Viability of a Palestinian State," *Journal of Palestine Studies,* 7 (Spring 1978).

_____ and Haim Darin-Drabkin. *Palestinian Independence — The Economic Aspect.* Tel-Aviv: no publisher, 1979 (Hebrew).

United Nations. *Report of the Commissioner-General of the United Nations Relief and Works Agency for Palestine Refugees in the Near East,* 1 July 1979–30 June 1980.

United States. Central Intelligence Agency. *National Basic Intelligence Factbook.* Washington, 1980.

_____ Department of State. *Bulletin.* Monthly.

_____ _____ *The Camp David Summit.* Publication 8954. Washington, 1978.

_____ Information Service. *United States Foreign Policy — Middle East: Basic Documents, 1950–1973.* Tel-Aviv: US Embassy, n.d.

_____ Library of Congress. Congressional Research Service. *West Bank and Gaza Economy: Problems and Prospects* (report prepared for US House of Representatives, Committee on Foreign Relations, Subcommittee on Europe and the Middle East). Reprinted in *Leviathan,* 3 (Fall 1980).

Van Arkadie, Brian. *Benefits and Burdens: A Report on the West Bank and Gaza Strip Economies Since 1967.* New York: Carnegie Endowment for International Peace, 1977.

Yorke, Valerie. "Palestinian Self-Determination and Israel's Security," *Journal of Palestine Studies,* 8 (Spring 1979).

Yusuf, Muhsin D. "The Potential Impact of Palestinian Education on a Palestinian State," *Journal of Palestine Studies,* 8 (Summer 1979).

Zack, Fredy. "The Development of Jenin in the Years 1967–1975," in *Judea and Samaria: Studies in Settlement Geography,* vol. II, ed. Avshalom Shmueli, David Grussman, and Rehavam Ze'evi. Jerusalem: Canaan Publishing, 1977 (Hebrew).

Index